W9-AHL-014

Librarians With Spines:

Information Agitators In An Age Of Stagnation, Vol. II

Edited by
Yago S. Cura
Max Macias

Library of Congress Catalonging-in-Publication Data
Yago Cura and Max Macias
Librarians with Spines: Information Agitators in an Age of Stagnation, Volume II
Includes bibliographical refrences and index
ISBN-978-1-7324848-2-5
Library of Congress Control Number: 2019938041

Copyrights

Editors: Yago Cura, Max Macias
Cover Design: Autumn Anglin
Interior Book Design: Autumn Anglin

© 2019 by Librarians with Spines: Information Agitators in an Age of Stagnation
Volume II
Los Angeles, California 90066

*All rights reserved. No part of theis book may be reproduced, in any form or by
any means, without permission in writing from the Editors.*

Book Printing Stats: Georgia, Helevetia
Printed and Bound by : Kindle Direct Publishing (KDP)

Printed in the United States of America

ISBN-978-1-7324848-2-5

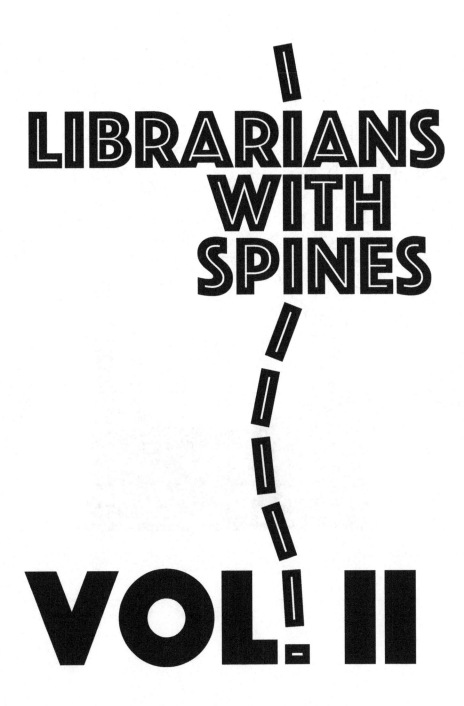

LIBRARIANS WITH SPINES

VOL. II

Artwork by Shanalee Hampton
www.shanaleehampton.com

Contents

Takeaways from the Hampton LIS Forum

Miguel Juárez, PhD, Jina DuVernay and Rebecca Hankins, CA

Above: Photograph by Crystal Burgoyne from the Families Together Rally, Salem Oregon, June 30, 2018, photograph used with permission .

Below: Photograph by Crystal Burgoyne from the Families Together Rally, Salem Oregon, June 30, 2018, photograph used with permission .

Preface

Miguel Juárez, Ph. D.
Rebecca Hankins, M.L.I.S., C.A.

What you hold in your hands is unlike anything you will read anytime soon. It is Yago S. Cura's and Max Macias' latest book Librarians with Spines: Information Agitators in An Age of Stagnation, Volume II! Theirs is a labor of love of bringing out progressive, alternative and radical voices in librarianship. Volume II adds to the diversity discourse in the library profession with co-edited essays from new voices. The six essays found in this volume reveal underlying issues which speak of other library histories which challenge the status quo and demonstrate that we have much work in our efforts towards democratizing information and addressing current socio-political issues in libraries, information science within the communities they serve. This text adds to the growing body of Critical Literature in Librarianship that challenges and confronts systems of oppression and control that undergird traditional information science work. These essays speak to what it takes to move from the supine to librarians with spines.

The American society is experiencing the year of immigration news, of detainment, of ICE raids, of the separation of children from their parents at the U.S./Mexico border, of increased threats to our fundamental civil rights. What is the role of libraries and librarians during these times, and what is that role? What are effective ways to center these issues, and who should take the lead? We have organizations that should take on leadership roles, but have they and why not? Where were the round tables like the Social Responsibilities Roundtable (SRRT); the Ethnic & Multicultural Information Exchange RT (EMIERT); the Gay, Lesbian, Bisexual, and Transgender Round Table (GLBTRT) and divisions like the Association of College & Research Libraries (ACRL); the Public Library Association (PLA) and other divisions; the Association of Research Libraries

(ARL)--have these groups publicly endorsed the LWS Series?

How can these often self-published works receive the publicity and exposure that ALA imprints garner? Cura and Macias have gone out on a quest to continue to push the envelope on crucial issues in librarianship. How do we challenge the narratives of inclusiveness and partner with the organizations and groups that seek to change the profession? Cura and Macias have had to fundraise and devote their time to publishing their series without much support, but their efforts benefit the entire information profession. This current volume speaks to the issues of diversity, inclusion, and representation and when work begins on Volume III we encourage other library organizations, who also have some skin in the game (and all do), step it up and collaborate with this outstanding series.

In his Introduction to *Volume II*, Dr. Jason K. Alston points out the lack of outlets to share his research on diversity. His study on Library Residency Program, which as of this printing, is the most thorough work was first ignored so he had to hustle to have his work supported through a variety of venues. Why is it that a finite number of authors find no problem being written up in the LIS professional publications while others have to hustle or seek other avenues to get their work recognized? Alston's essay leads us to the important question, what if the LWS Series did not exist? Would any of the contributors in this volume have been published?

In this current age of the delegitimating facts Grace Yamada, in her important chapter: "Digital Citizenship in its Second Decade: An Examination and a Way Forward," outlines the urgent work of schools "incorporating more digital concepts and themes into their curriculums, programs and conversations."[1] According to Yamada, there is a need to teach digital literacy to library patrons, students and colleagues and libraries, and as early adopters, libraries provide the foundation for that learning.[2]

A May 31, 2019 IFLA Communications email detailed the urgency of the issue, "In 2015 the United Nations agreed to a 2030 Agenda that specifically underlined the importance of access to information as a driver of development. The 2019 IFLA President's Meeting, held in Buenos Aires, Argentina on 23 May, explored how libraries, as guarantors of this access, can be motors of change,

---

1 Grace Yamada, "Digital Citizenship in its Second Decade: An Examination and a Way Forward," in Yago S. Cura and Max Macias, *Librarians With Spines, Volume II*. Los Angeles: Hinchas Press, 2019, 2.

2 Ibid., 4-5.

and saw a call to action to all participating, in person and online... Those who have access and the skills to use it are able to take seize opportunities, take better decisions and innovate. Those without risk being left behind."[3] LWS has answered the call with the mission to provide access to those vulnerable and marginalized populations. Yago S. Cura's and Max Macias' *Librarians with Spines Volume II* is blazing a trail that serves as a model for more librarians, archivists, and other information professionals to add to the literary canon.

---

3 International Federation of Library Administrations (IFLA) Communications, email Friday, May 31, 2019 at 8:24 am. [IFLA-L] IFLA President's Meeting 2019: New Perspectives, New Possibilities and a Call to Action for Libraries as Motors of Change

Photograph by Crystal Burgoyne from the Families Together Rally, Salem Oregon, June 30, 2018, photograph used with permission .

Introduction
Jason K. Alston

Perhaps the greatest honor I will receive this year was my invitation from Yago Cura and Max Macias to pen the introduction to the second volume of Librarians with Spines. In the first volume, Yago and Max gifted me with an opportunity to write some thoughts I had harbored for a long time regarding the five library ethnic caucuses. Before that, I had had no venue to express these ideas. I consider my contribution to the first installment of Librarians with Spines a success, and believe the first volume, as a whole to have been a game-changing contribution to library literature.

Originally, I intended to contribute a chapter to this volume you hold in your hands; it would have been an opinionated chapter based on my research on diversity residency programs. As you can imagine, there are quite a few things that I need to say to add meaning to the data I collected. After publishing my dissertation, I reached out to a popular library news outlet that publishes stories daily to ask if they would be interested in "running" a story about my research. I was told by this outlet, whom I feel no need to identify, that they had already run a news item before describing what diversity residencies were. It seemed lost on this library news outlet that new and interesting information about something they had already once reported on just might one day surface. And despite the fact that treatment of diversity residents in our field was and still is a pressing diversity concern within our field, they had no interest in doing even a brief story on my research.

Even though I had completed the largest study ever done on diversity residency programs, and the research I had completed had the potential to inform practice, my research was of no interest to an outlet that needs to find news stories

every day? There are only a handful of empirical research studies on diversity residency programs in existence, even though diversity residency programs have existed at least since 1984. So I continued to "shop" my research, hoping that eventually someone would take interest in it. That finally happened during a chance encounter with a faculty member from the School of Information Sciences at the University of Tennessee, Knoxville. UTK thankfully gave me a platform to discuss my findings, and from there, my research gained more attention than I could have ever dreamed.

The attention my research garnered has been a blessing and a curse. I see now, more than ever, how starved this field continues to be for research and discourse concerning diversity issues. I have been asked to speak at multiple venues, collaborate on additional research, and publish in a variety of media due to my findings. However, the cost has been overcommitment and an inability to contribute to some projects that I find to be particularly important, such as Volume 2 of Librarians with Spines. Even my performance at my day job has suffered, as I have failed to establish the proper balance between pushing diversity research and optimally serving my current employer, and thus students, in day-to-day operations.

The editors of this book have sacrificed their time, money, and standing to grow and build their benevolent library work. They, too, have been "stonewalled" by library news outlets that did not understand the gravity of this type of work, but they pressed on, as will the rest of us. It may in fact be these similar, shared sacrifices that strengthen our resolve to work together as we tirelessly nourish this field, even if detractors say they do not want to hear it, and tell us they've heard enough of it.

There is something to be said about how being told what you do is of no value brings people together. Being told the work I was doing was not important brought me, a Black practitioner from the east coast into forming such a bond with Yago and Max, two Latino librarians grinding it out on the west coast. And dismissal of similar concerns is possibly what brought a standing-room-only crowd to the "Librarians with Spines" panel held during the third Joint Librarians of Color Conference including n 2018. Just minutes before our panel began--which featured myself and several of the contributors to the first volume of Librarians with Spines--I remember having concerns that possibly no one would attend.

Instead, we were greeted by a packed room. I am prone to believe that many of those who attended had their own experiences with being dismissed or trivialized when raising diversity of identity issues within the library profession. Diana Lopez, Mary Rayme, Yago and myself captivated the audience before us, simply because they could relate.

That is the power of Librarians with Spines. Along with all the contributors to this current volume, and to my colleagues in the previous volume, we are those librarians who keep standing when attempts are made to knock us down and keep us pinned.

From Left: Yago Cura, Jason Alston, Mary Reyme and Diana Lopez, at the JCLC, 3rd National Joint Confreence of Librarians of Color, on Friday Sept 28, 2018 1:45 PM - 3:00 PM in Santo Domingo, as our panel for Librarians With Spines.

Above: Photograph by Crystal Burgoyne from the Families Together Rally, Salem Oregon, June 30, 2018, photograph used with permission .

Below: Photograph by Crystal Burgoyne from the Families Together Rally, Salem Oregon, June 30, 2018, photograph used with permission .

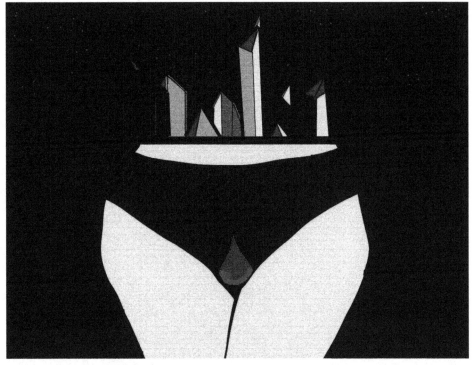

"I created "Period Piece" during my last menstrual cycle, wanting to explore my feelings about menstruation through art which I'd never done before. Much of the art I've seen on the topic of menstruation has been pretty similar in theme- pink, white and red. Cute flowers and cartoons. Memes about chocolate. Just hashtag #periodart for reference. I get it, but I don't identify with it. I wanted to represent my reality with it. Menstruation for me, who is also battling with MS, means that no matter how much I to boost my immune system, I'm going to get sick. I'll likely have several days of throbbing migraines and ridiculously painful cramps along with an MS flare up. Included with those issues are insomnia and stomach problems. And I'm an emotional mess of anxiety from both MS and PMDD. I meditate, take the supplements, the epsom soaks, do all of the things... but it always seems to win.

Social media wants to normalize periods, and I do too! But I think that normalization should include more than pink and flowers. I think my depiction is accurate for many. Menstruation can be a dark and painful place to be, and that is ok.

It's a time to connect with the body in an especially magical way, even if that magic is simply crafted by beating that darkness one month at a time."

-Amy Willis

https://www.libidobidil.com/

Digital Citizenship in its Second Decade: An Examination and a Way Forward

Grace Yamada

Abstract

Digital Citizenship, the concept that we take our civic responsibilities and rights to online spaces, has exploded into public consciousness. Many librarians, particularly those that work with youth such as myself, are scrambling to incorporate more digital citizenship concepts and themes into their curriculums, programs and conversations. The wave of interest began several years ago (digital citizenship regularly appearing on 'hot trends' in education lists) and continues to the present moment. When a report from NPR in 2016 circulated stating that only 20% of young Americans could identify false information online, panic about information and digital literacy came to the library. Educators, librarians and parents had clearly failed to teach the skills American kids and teens needed. This begged the question, what didn't we teach and why? The trouble is that there is very little clarity about what exactly digital citizenship encompasses and how to instruct and model good citizenship to patrons, students and colleagues. By tracing the development of the term, I hope to provide a usable, teachable definition with practical examples. Recent polling shows that the public trusts and relies on libraries and librarians more than ever; it is incumbent that librarians are prepared to explain what it means to be a tech-user today, and positively influence the online landscape of the future.

Digital Citizenship, the concept that we take our civic responsibilities and rights to online spaces, has exploded into public consciousness. Heightened interest in the state of both online and offline discourse may seem sudden due to recent political events as calls for 'civility' echo uselessly around the online and offline world. Concern regarding digital responsibility is not new; however, recent events in politics, technology and culture have turned the spotlight on online behavior and how it affects us in 'real' life. As CEOs are called upon to answer for their platform's contribution to the world information economy, we realize that the rules of engagement have never been clear and the responsibility of appropriate and progressive technology use has fallen on the individual. In most cases, that individual is neither prepared nor protected in the endeavor to use and improve the digital world. As governments, activists, teachers and families publicly struggle with questions of access, responsibility and control, librarians and information workers should integrate community-minded ideals into how they ask patrons to use the Internet (Searson, Hancock, Soheil & Shepherd, 2015). As a professional community we should teach and model civically engaged Internet use that acknowledges the wide array of experiences online and seeks digital equity for all.

As we set standards for young, old, inexperienced and vulnerable patrons we should use accessible, correct language to teach wise online habits that can make the Internet a better place for everyone. Libraries should integrate ethical considerations into their technology instruction, both formally and informally (Atif & Chien, 2018). Librarians can intervene when they see patrons are confused or concerned by validating their fears and offering resources to protect and help them. For example, if a patron sets a password that is easy to guess or otherwise insecure, a librarian can intervene and suggest a better strategy for passwords and talk about why. With this relatively low effort from the librarian, the patron can get practical help that they may be able to apply in the future. As with other social services that fall on libraries by default, the burden of getting underserved people access and providing adequate education and support for healthy online life falls on library staff and is expected of us (Geiger, 2017). I hope that a discussion of the history of digital citizenship and a conversation about how we can improve our own practice in its context, mostly in terms of language, will instill interest and provide tools for library staff everywhere.

Libraries of all kinds can act as a foundational space and early adopters of not only digital and technological access, but civic life and culture. They also have a long and storied history of being early technology adopters, and an equally long history of providing access to this material to their neighborhoods and communities. For many, it is one of the few places to use computers to access the Internet for free. Americans on the whole use libraries regularly, and generally have positive feelings towards them (Zickuhr, Rainie & Purcell, 2013). With such privilege and trust, it would behoove the profession as a whole and individuals participating in the information market to consider our role in digital culture and its relationship to digital equity. While not all libraries and staff have the access and support they need to develop and teach best practices to others, we can and should play an integral role in shaping the public conversation about what the Internet could be through example and instruction as much as we are able.

A thorough and nuanced understanding of the impact of what digital citizenship is and could be will help librarians contribute to the continuing history of the term and concept to the advantage of our communities we serve. This is a natural role for libraries and their staff, whose existence and organization has always been tied to the information technology available. Polling shows that public trust in libraries as neutral and safe repositories of information and research is at an all-time high (Geiger, 2017). Some writers have even upheld librarians' expert knowledge of databases and sources as an alternative to deeply suspect search engines and advertisement-riddled web browsers (Noble, 2018). Information institutions and professionals should feel motivated and be supported in their efforts to understand digital citizenship and guide the conversation. Librarians can directly challenge preconceived notions of who and what matters online with programming and conversation. They can educate their patrons about the changes that may come to and through technology with their specific communities in mind.

Many librarians, particularly those that work with youth such as myself, are scrambling to incorporate more digital citizenship concepts and themes into their curriculums, programs and conversations. The noticeable intensifying wave of interest began several years ago when digital citizenship regularly started appearing on 'hot trends' in education lists on blogs and websites targeting educators and continues to the present moment. When a report from NPR in 2016 circulated stating that only a fraction of young Americans, middle school to college, could identify false information online, panic came to the library. The trouble is that there is very little clarity about what exactly digital and literacy citizenship encompass.

Without this framework of history and ideals librarians are unable to instruct and model good digital citizenship to patrons, students and colleagues. We cannot project optimism about the future of digital society without the foundation of a philosophy based in civically engaged Internet use. By tracing the development of the term, I hope to provide a usable, teachable definition that will empower librarians of all kinds to pass on the knowledge and protection of digital citizenship.

History

As a concept, citizenship itself is immensely complicated. Its origins are widely disputed and its development is just as controversial. What scholars and textbooks can agree on is that citizenship is a state of belonging to a body beyond kinship. Citizenship typically requires some political participation and entitles an individual to rights. Despite attempts to provide basic and permanent rights based on nationality or residency, there is a wide range of privileges attached to citizenship. Furthermore, the supposed benefits of citizenship are not bestowed equally, automatically or all at once (Finlayson, 2005). As marginalized populations across global history agitate for full protections of citizenship they encounter state-sponsored cultural and legal barriers to citizenships as well as violence.

As we consider digital citizenship, it is helpful to remember the complex and continuing sociopolitical issues surrounding the term and concept. With this context and history in mind, librarians should approach digital citizenship with the intent to avoid the racism, sexism and other prejudices that have prevented people from attaining the full benefits of citizenship and online life. Using concepts like digital citizenship and digital equity can help provoke a digital awareness by communicating the rights that each individual has online. This can increase civic engagement, spread economic opportunity and promote a true state of belonging (Mossberger, Tolbert & McNeal, 2010). Digital citizenship sits awkwardly in the lineage of the development of citizenship, (generally) divorced from physical place and a state-granted passport. A history of access to the technology and Internet shows that 'digital citizenship' suffers from the same inequality and lack of access as many other types of citizenship. In order to situate digital citizenship as a worthy goal for communities in and out of the library, professionals and institutions must prove that digital citizenship will benefit patrons in tangible ways.

Clearly, the phrase 'digital citizens' evokes legality, geographical place and sovereignty in a manner unwieldy for the Internet: a placeless place that exists in signal bounced from server to server around (and off) the world. This particular form of citizenship does not always need a physical nation to reside in. It can be carried on a device in a library card and citizens of the same digital communities do not need to share common passports, language or hold the same rights. Citizenship without nationality functions within a set of expectations that prioritize a bond other than shared nationality. As such, digital citizenship will need a more proactive understanding of technology in society as well as individuals who can self-select into their communities.

Digital citizenship as a concept emerged in the late nineties and early aughts, at least in professional literature targeting students and teachers in the United States. The International Society for Technology in Education released a two-page 'Standard for Students' in 1998 outlining the attributes of a technology literate student. Their requirements include 'Social Ethical and Human Issues' and later in the document 'Technology Problem-solving and Decision-making Tools' which provide a loose blueprint for the literature that was to come. A brief article from 2004 defines digital citizenship as "norms of behavior" when interacting with technology. This early view into the perception of society online is enlightening and concerning. It shows the divergence of an offline citizen and an online one: namely that while citizenship is a privilege that comes with responsibility, online citizenship is merely abiding by 'norms'. The authors identify plagiarizing, cell phone and gaming device use in class, blackmail and more as examples of technology abuse. While these issues are doubtless serious, particularly for young people in classrooms, policing norms is the beginning of what an active digital citizen should be (Searson, Hancock, Soheil & Shepherd, 2015).

In the decade since then, norms about when technology is appropriate have changed quite a bit. Schools are adding technology to classrooms instead of limiting it both institutionally and through 'bring your own device' programs. Libraries have consistently added tools, devices and programming that help their patrons use the internet since the early days of personal computers and demand has only gone up since then (Horrigan, 2016). With initiatives like hotspot lending, which allows patrons to borrow a Wi-Fi device; libraries have affirmed that providing Internet access is a service they want to provide. The rising concern about digital citizenship for students can be attributed in part at least, to the spread of social media. In terms of platforms like Snapchat, Facebook and others are becoming so integral to recreational culture that they are no longer recreational but necessary for some commerce and organizing (Mossberger, Tolbert & McNeal, 2010).

Other articles from 2004 report on schools using digital citizenship as a framework to instill the importance of respecting copyright; in other words, preserving ownership standards from one format to another. Repeated themes in the early professional literature aimed at youth educators are interruptions to education, misuse of devices and lack of etiquette when using the web (Ribble & Bailey, 2004). This approach to acclimating people to the web does not truly address the definitional core of citizenship, which implies participation in a community as an agent for good. If we consider digital citizenship in the context of history, the fundamental purpose should be to emphasize the rights and protections of communities.

While mentions of personal freedom, community and learning are present in the texts I encountered, they are generally couched in language that implies an economic contract with the Internet and personal devices. One oft-cited article even refers to students as 'stakeholders' (Altınay Gazi, Z. 2016). Literature that does expand the concept beyond 'don't break rules' does so briefly with none of the urgency that it uses when addressing copyright infractions.

In 2007, the International Society for Technology in Education, a global technology resource for educators, added digital citizenship as one of six standards of technology in education. ISTE's definition includes responsible information use, personal commitment to learning and leadership in the online and technological sphere. Since then, there have been various handbooks published for librarians and teachers, mostly with juvenile populations. The focus on cyberbullying is consistent in this literature, again mostly aimed at teachers and students in primary education. Digital Citizenship week was founded in 2013 by Common Sense Media, a nonprofit most famous for rating recreational media for parents concerned about adult content in television and movies. This yearly spotlight on digital citizenship is representative of these initiatives that generally include resources for teachers that help classes think through when and how they use technology. Common Sense Media's effort to help parents and schools raise smart, responsible and respectful technology users is laudable, but limiting in their focus on schools and children when digital citizenship is challenging and an evolving concept for all ages and in many places.

Digital citizenship was most prominently mentioned in legislation when the United States Congress updated the Children's Protection Act (CIPA) from 2001. This law stipulates that schools must teach "appropriate online behavior (building a positive digital footprint; respecting intellectual property), safety and privacy, and cyberbullying awareness and response" in order to receive funding. In 2001 CIPA survived a constitutional challenge from the American Library Association and the American Civil Liberties Union, who believed CIPA would make the digital divide worse. In 2017, the Washington State Senate passed Bill 5449 that instructs educators and librarians to assess their digital citizenship and online safety curriculums and ultimately create a best practices document that will act as a standard for schools and libraries in the state. Both of these legal documents identify cyberbullying as a central catalyst to their creation.

Today, the study and implementation of digital citizenship has been revitalized by the focus on online life for a variety of reasons, all of them negative. The spread of deliberately misleading information, online tribalism, interference in democratic processes worldwide, death and sexual assault, bullying, massive hacks and much more racist, sexist and generally bad behavior online is common. An alarming and widely shared article from NPR in 2017 cited a Stanford study of over 7,000 students, middle school to college age, finding most young Americans unable to differentiate between sponsored content and legitimate news (Domonoske, 2016). Perhaps inadvertently, the panic around this study scapegoated young Americans for a political atmosphere that they had nothing to do with and which is immensely complicated. Educators and librarians have been called upon to fill in the digital literacy gaps that have grown even as access and usage rates have risen.

Now, digital literacy along with digital citizenship is a concern for adults, not just children and students. Using the Internet is not age-restricted (in reality) and the onus for good behavior and enforcing social boundaries does not fall on those 18 or younger alone. Recently, we have been confronted with how uneducated the vast majority of Americans are regarding their relationship to online platforms and in turn, how little control we have over digital culture.

The Digital Divide

Technology, its spread and use, has been heralded the great leveler of peoples. No matter who you are, goes this line of thinking, you can use the Internet to create music, start a business or make money and gain recognition. Despite the many examples of Internet-generated wealth in many demographics, this optimism seems unwarranted (Joint, 2005). The landmark study conducted by the National Telecommunications and Information Administration in 1998 was the first national study to record and study Internet use. They found that while Internet use continued to rise, both race and class divided the most and least connected citizens. Furthermore, the gap in access and ownership was getting bigger over time. This phenomenon, named the "digital divide" by the founder of the Markle Foundation in 2000, is now widely studied by library, educational and information professionals. The Merriam-Webster dictionary defines the Digital Divide as "the economic, educational, and social inequalities between those who can access computers and the Internet and those who do not." This definition is merely the tip of the iceberg when it comes to lack of online and technology access that includes not only access but also technical skills. Basic skills like how to click a mouse, use a search engine or login to an email account need to be taught, as well as how to identify an ad, check dates on articles and how to avoid digital thieves of all kinds. Having access to the Internet (whether someone owns a personal computer or not) is the first step to a fulfilling, civic digital life. This person must also have skills to navigate their technology; without it, we cannot truly consider these patrons on the right side of the digital divide (van Deursen & van Dijk, 2010). The concept of the digital divide has developed in the two decades since it was coined--moving from ownership and access to control and self-determination. With this history and the development of digital citizenship in mind, the standards of digital participation need examination, expansion and promotion. The previous emphasis on youth populations ignored the technology users over 18-- perhaps the more influential segment of web-users who also needed a social framework to function within.

As librarians, teachers and information professionals are trying to confront misleading information packaged to spread as quickly as possible, we are confronted with what digital citizenship means to us as professionals, individuals and representatives of our various institutions. Librarians should take this opportunity to elevate participation in online life and strengthen social bonds online that can propel digital equity forward. Through conversation, programs and curriculum we should move away from sovereignty-based notions of citizenship towards a view of Internet participation focused on understanding the Internet both technically and culturally. In order to assert legal rights for people online and promote equity in the digital sphere communities should create policies and norms that protect and promote their information needs in the most natural of civic spaces, the library.

Neither the aggressive anti-piracy stance, nor the bullying prevention-focused position fully captures the scope of what a digital citizenship could be. More educators and information professionals should reevaluate digital citizenship with ethics and inclusivity in mind as their patrons and students enter the online world. A digital citizen must navigate contentious waters, but a more holistic concept of what it means to use the web can help combat issues in the field and create technology users who are smart enough to protect themselves and others in their online communities.

Implementation

I propose that digital citizenship is membership in a forward-looking community that emphasizes self-awareness and promotes thoughtful engagement on the Internet as creators as well as consumers. Part of self-awareness requires a historical understanding of the privileged nature of access and acknowledging the different experiences of marginalized patrons. A static list of rules will become obsolete quickly, but a philosophy that promotes digital citizenship could transform confusion and fear into action and empowerment. The overall framework should generate awareness about the lack of digital equity, technical knowledge and teaching and modeling good digital citizenship. This means we must build the unmapped nature of the web into our technology instruction and including the overlooked or erased contribution to the development of the Internet as we know it. Digital citizens should also consider themselves part of a global network that encompasses people who do not look or sound like them. Introducing and expanding patrons, students and others' identity from 'user' to 'citizen' means learners should be encouraged to be critical of the rules--written and unwritten-- that govern the world of technology.

In my own work as public librarian, I see the attitude that posits that if you do nothing wrong you will be safe. This passive and damaging mindset should be replaced with active participation will keep a patron informed enough to make good decisions concerning their own digital citizenship. While some users and establishments would like to rely on corporations and institutions to informally or formally regulate acceptable practices online, a wealth of research shows that technology, especially automation, can be used against citizens as often as for their benefit. Consider illegal surveillance of activists or weaponized automation of healthcare and welfare. Teaching someone how to live and be on the Internet is a thorny path; a librarian must instill values of self-awareness and the importance of information to help or hurt.

My information literacy instruction forefronts the diverse and messy conception of the Internet. Changing attitudes about technology is an uphill climb. In my experience there is no one demographic that can be blamed for bad habits, poor skills and resistance to improvement. By using more inclusive and accurate language librarians can create opportunities to teach and learn about the Internet and technology in patron-focused, community-specific ways. When I facilitate technology, game design and coding programs we discuss the value of self-expression, invention and using technology to solve problems in our communities. When we accept individual responsibility for creating a community of access, inclusion and progress we can experience technology beyond the sleek white boxes of capitalism.

In everyday librarianship demands on time, budget and emotion are almost endless. Librarians are increasingly asked to take on more and a wider variety of work and informally act as people who can soothe anxieties and provide emotional support while facilitating information-seeking activities. This is particularly true of inexperienced web-users who rely on the library as their primary Internet access point. Digital citizenship is especially important to the vulnerable and people unversed in the unwritten rules of online life. By presenting the Internet as space where there are rights and obligations, a librarian can instill values and educate at the same time. The often-heralded significance of privacy and cyberbullying are just as important to adult users of the web as they are for minors and students. Digital citizenship can prevent exploitation by specifying the rights inherent in membership to that community.

Understanding digital citizenship is essential to instilling wise information habits in patrons who trust library staff or information workers to educate and guide them online. Overall, librarianship embraces the potential of the Internet to help people learn, connect, be creative and engage the world for leisure and profit. Librarians should also educate their patrons about their personal freedoms and responsibilities on the Internet as well as the history of those rights and dangers to them. In order to improve the online experience for everyone, particularly the marginalized and inexperienced patrons we serve, every librarian should consider their own practices and how to improve them. This could include evaluating the tools they recommend and the language they teach with when contextualizing Internet use in the library. Through conversation, example and instruction, librarians can embody technology-positive, inclusive and empathetic attitudes that influence the future of the Internet.

Above: Photograph by Crystal Burgoyne from the Families Together Rally, Salem Oregon, June 30, 2018, photograph used with permission .

Below: Photograph by Crystal Burgoyne from the Families Together Rally, Salem Oregon, June 30, 2018, photograph used with permission .

Senior Citizen Zinesters

Yago Cura

I. "Essence Rare" of Zines

"I found that essence rare, it's what I looked for/ I knew I'd get what I asked for"

--Gang of Four, "I Found that Essence Rare"

Zines seem the province of the young and dynamic because they're somewhat indefinable, and at the same time slightly unpronounceable. I mean, is it zeens? Is it zhines? (How could I possibly maneuver a form I can't even pronounce?) According to Chip Rowe in "The Book of Zines: Readings from the Fringe" (1997) zines are "self-published magazines reproduced...on the sly and distributed through mail order and word of mouth." (xii). Zines are homemade books or pamphlets: impromptu manuscripts obsessed with "sex, music, politics, television, movies, word, food, whatever." (Rowe, xii). They owe a debt to "Dadaists, science fiction fans, anarchists, poets, and other self-starters, along with the technology such as the mimeograph" (Rowe, xii). Therefore, any magazine or book fashioned at home, and covering any subject, and distributed by its creator through the mail or dispensed by hand is a zine.

"Zines were around in the fifties and sixties and then punk rock and its Do-It-Yourself aesthetic pushed them along in the seventies. The arrival of self-service copiers and desktop publishing did the same in the eighties" (Rowe, xii). Regardless of the era, the essence of zines seems nebulous because they are de facto restless emanations, energized by the ubiquity of the now. Part confessional, part journal, the potential threat zines pose remains immediacy-of-message, exponentially duplicated: an urgency that's hard to match and extremely easy to duplicate. This keeps the stakes of actually making a zine relatively low, but laden with idiosyncrasies. There are no ugly or inconsequential zines, but not all zines are created equal; the effort behind any zine's pages is always entirely evident, always obvious, and is especially difficult to fake.

As early as 1994, the LA Times were reporting on zines as portals to youth culture, "self-published glimpses into the lives of twentysomethings" (La Ganga, par. 1). The mimeographed aesthetics of zines are decidedly not for everyone, especially those that believe it takes "talent" to create a homemade book, or those morbidly afraid of toner. But the prevailing logic is that anyone can make a zine, and well, for years, those "anyones" have been "The often twentysomething publishers...carrying on a conversation at once both public and private[,] and doing it in intimate print-a-medium." (La Ganga, par. 9). However, the "essence rare" of zines is that zines engender community. You might even say that zines are like little community turbines.

As soon as you make a zine, you are admitted into the class of "zinester," regardless of affiliation, creed, weight, credit score, or sexual orientation. It's not that simply by making a zine you will be granted admittance into Xerox-Valhalla, but making a zine is kind of like joining the mailing list at your favorite record shop or bookstore. You, your contact information exists in time and space through your "being"; somewhere out there, in the wide world of mailing lists there is a slot with your name and email on it. Making zines is not just about folding paper and airing intimate thoughts, but also about the connections and networks that sharing--that is, distributing--those zines create. In that same 1994 LA Times article, R. Seth Friedman, "publisher of Factsheet 5" (par. 24) and the Zeus of Zines, explained that "They [zines] are an egalitarian and accessible form of communication designed... by people who feel isolated and want to connect." (par 31). In very real terms, a zinester is someone who feels unheard, unappreciated and unwilling to take no for an answer and knows the person with the keys (or the code) to the copier room.

The other thing about zines is that they "crush" minutiae, meaning they commit "to paper the details of daily life in the late 20th century, an era devoid of the 'personal documentation' that crowds libraries and provides the raw material of history." (La Gange, par. 10) In an era increasingly about the reduction of paper and mediating the limitations of our memory, both in our minds and on our devices, zines provide messy, obsessive indexing, proof, signs of life--receipts--that document the ecosystem of lifestyles that exist in a milieu built on magnetic tape. Zines are not only primary sources, that is, 21st century documents made in the 21st century, "zines are [also] the sotto voce version--filled with the sort of information formerly penned within the impervious walls of friendship and family." (La Ganga, par. 8). Zines integrate various artistic techniques (collage, bricolage, assemblage) before they even hit the pane of the Xerox machine, and require time to construct. Zinesters typically carry their zines-in-production around like some talisman: working on it on their time off from their cubicle, or scribbling on it when things gets boring at the sex shop, or when they have some downtime.

Zines are personalized, inaudible morsels that crumble off after eating big meals comprised of heartache, identity, the heartache over identity, idiosyncrasy-

-they all get equal screen time with zines; as such, the reader "get[s] all the dirty office gossip without any of the involvement" (La Ganga, par. 14). So, wouldn't it be folly to believe that identity, obsession, and ennui should exclusively be spent on the young and morose when we can work with nascent octogenarian zinesters who have been cultivating these pillars since before the Great Wars? Imagine all the little gripes that might aggregate during a lifetime. Put those in the severed-brake-line-mouth of a person in their 80's, and you just might have the platonic ingredients for a Zinester.

II. Vitamin Sotto Voce

"People say that we're crazy/ We're sick and all alone/ But when we read your letters we're rolling on the floor"

-- Dead Kennedys, "Stealing People's Mail"

As early as January of 2011, the Pew Research Center was estimating that, "...[every day]... for the next 19 years, 10,000 baby boomers will reach age 65." ("Baby Boomers..."). Furthermore, "By 2030, when all members of the Baby Boom generation have reached that age, fully 18% of the nation will be at least that age." ("Baby Boomers..."). Indeed, as Baby Boomers begin to retire in increasing numbers, it stands to reason that the numbers of senior adults entering Senior Housing and Independent Living Centers will increase substantially as well. Senior homes and independent living facilities might be heavy on interaction, but that doesn't mean they automatically satisfy those seeking community. Regardless of the setting, it always takes awhile to find your pack or coven or rabble. You could be surrounded by peers and acquaintances and still feel like the lighthouse operator of a very sad bay. In other words, by 2030 almost a fifth of the U.S. population is set to retire, and regardless of where they land they are going to want programming-- and they are going to want it yesterday, you lollygagger!

What benefits might residents in assisted-living facilities enjoy by sitting down once a week with other residents to create zines? Could making zines with senior citizens help reduce the symptoms associated with dementia and Alzheimer's, despite obvious pathological differences? In her 2006 article in the LA Times, "The Healing Canvas: Art can soothe the mind and body, therapists say. Now science backs them up", Jenny Hontz cites a "...Northwestern Memorial Hospital study of

50 men and women...[that]...found...an hour of art therapy significantly reduced a broad spectrum of cancer-related symptoms such as pain, anxiety, exhaustion, depression, loss of appetite and shortness of breath." (par. 7). On Oct. 26, 2018 the Journals of Gerontology published a study that transpired at FSU's College of Medicine conducted by Dr. Angelina R. Sutin, Dr. Yannick Stephan, Dr. Martina Luchetti, and Dr. Antonio Terracciano, in which they found that "loneliness was associated with a 40% increased risk of dementia." The physical act of crafting a zine might be a cost-effective way of resuscitating parts of the brain that dampen with age; it might even be a quick and convenient way to stave off dementia and senility, or at least provide a way to slow early onset Alzheimer's.

Doesn't it make sense to "standardize" this type of art therapy with older adults by enticing our public libraries to engage with Senior Houses and Independent Living Centers to "roll" programs out on a national level? Could cheap, brain-resuscitating, zine programming help the senior citizens in our country age in a more humane way? Might the manual tasks involved in constructing a zine (not just folding paper, but cutting images out of magazines, and coloring) prove moderate panacea for seniors experiencing mobility issues, or healing from a particularly nasty tumble? Last, in what ways do zines allow zinesters--regardless of age--the latitude to not only share their ideas, memories, and secret stirrings, but to curate them for small groups? Zines archive our waking moments of industrious clarity, and allow us to discover an instantaneous forum (and form).

III. Constellations of Mistakes

"Because there's 40 different shades of black/

So many fortresses and ways to attack"

-- Pavement, "Elevate Me Later"

Crafting zines can lend several marked advantages to literacy efforts with any demographic, but the most integral advantage remains creation of community. The creation and distribution of zines promises a particularly convenient way for residents in senior homes and independent living facilities to participate in palliative art workshops, while at the same time assisting library systems with their efforts to recycle old journals and magazines by providing potential zinesters fodder for zines. A zine session for senior citizens would not be more expensive or time-consuming than for any other group or demographic; the therapy it would provide for senior citizens could enhance the way we age, along with amplifying the parameters of what we consider community.

Since August 2018, I have conducted zine workshops at senior living facilities and independent living centers on the westside of Los Angeles. Typically, a zine workshop lasts for at least an hour; because we are working with senior citizens, many of whom might have physical challenges, it makes sense to build in at least a two-hour workshop. "Grazing" over old magazines and journals, and chewing the proverbial cud, (chusmeando) are part and parcel of the experience. The more relaxed you are about facilitating the workshop and the entire program, the more organic and unexpected the entire endeavor becomes. I might even suggest absolutely no constraints as to theme, subject, or perspective to get started, and then induce those conceits and protocols later on in the trajectory of the program. In one class, I attempted to "rebrand" my zine workshop as a "memoir-trading book workshop" in which participants would select one moment in their life and write out and illustrate the integral plot points. This type of prompting or "easing" works if the template or prompt you have created is the final zine. The senior citizen zinesters I worked with had little to no interest in transferring material from the pre-folded templates onto blank zine "canvases".

I would also suggest demonstrating what an "interesting" image might be for you, the facilitator; that is, show the seniors how to rip out, cut, and select--and thus crop--potential zine images from the pages of magazines like People, Time and Us. As the facilitator, and to save time, you could "make it rain" pictures-- snippets of glossy magazine images, cut-outs, newsprint columns, etc.--that you have pre-cut in the middle of the table, and allow the senior zinesters to grab/ utilize whatever image they wanted and that was available--whatever caught their eye. However, you run the risk of overly prompting participants into creating proxy zines that are really variations of your style, or the things that caught your particular eye.

Facilitators can also just place supplies on the table innocuously, in little "stations" that contain like things. For example, I make a station for scissors, one for glue, and fashion several "piles" of images for participants to rifle through before sitting down to my own process. "Here is a pile of cut-out cats from a cat calendar...there are some newspaper columns from Sunday's Times...over here is a pile of pics of Dwayne Johnson. And this, this is a manual for a defunct toaster oven." Just remember, you must submit to the process, the process of making a zine "on the spot" just like your students. Do not expect to escape the anxiety of the white page simply because you are wearing the facilitator hat. That's not how zines work. Facilitating a zine workshop is not like leading a Master's class or reading a lecture from the "cover" of a lectern. There is no such thing as a zine teacher; the only real thing a facilitator conducting a zine workshop can do is initiate the process and guide novice zinesters.

The facilitator must sit down with a blank 6-fold zine and create a zine in front of participants. Entice them to paste, stick, and caption images with whatever text they might be able to score. During a particularly productive workshop, I made a zine and christened it "Podium" by stenciling those words on the cover. Also on the cover, a photo of LBJ mobbed by pixels of people, thousands of people, and he is facing the camera which is behind the podium—hence the title. I have attached it as a jpeg and a pdf so that it can be printed, manipulated or changed (*See Appendix A*). The workshop where I created this zine was magical; participants were able to see the crafting of a zine from start to finish, from cover image to captions and stenciling.

While sorting and cutting out images, my senior citizen zinesters and I talked about marriage and raising kids and the challenges of sustaining a house and a marriage while working full-time. As the facilitator, I had not given them a theme, subject, or perspective; yet participants picked up scissors, or rifled through piles, or ransacked the enormous Zip-Lock bag that contained the zine supplies completely of their own volition. It was almost as if they were searching for supplies for a blueprint that was adroitly nebulizing into view, but that had yet to be born in time and space. It was kind of revelatory in that I did not supply a mission, and yet this was not busy work because the interest was completely self-directed. It might help to include pictures of cats and dogs, because every demographic feels a certain way about cats and dogs. Stencils of varying font sizes are also helpful. Remember, a zine workshop is like a kitchen sink omelet: the components might be leftovers or the remnants of a half-eaten doggy bag, but once they are compiled onto the pages of a zine, they begin to take on their own narrative and begin to seethe with possibilities.

During the initial zine workshop, you will definitely want to show participants how to make a 6-fold zine, along with discussing the various other formats and paper lengths of zines. It would be wise to talk about the merits that imperfections lend to the production. It is advisable that facilitators discuss the zine's history as a homemade book made by "ardent science fiction fans in the 1950's" (La Ganga, par. 13) because most senior citizen zinesters would have been alive during that time and could be familiar with zines, or at least this schema. It might also prove advantageous to prompt participants about the importance of collage, bricolage, and assemblage, as well as repetition. There are so many methods to approach the production of zines that picking one might seem a daunting task. As the facilitator, you will be expected to have a plan of attack. You are the guide; participants will expect you to steer them through the landscape of zine production (and hold their hands a little). The difficult part is allowing the zines to be imperfect, to be half-wrought and stilted. The difficult part is extending the production past the initial workshop or two. Getting buy-in from the seniors you are working with is integral to facilitating more workshops so that additional techniques can be disseminated.

By the end of the first workshop, participants should know how to fold a 6-fold zine (*See Appendix B*), and determine the zine's pagination. A 6-fold zine has six pages, along with a cover and a back cover--eight pages total. It might be a good idea to use page one in a 6-fold zine as the colophon, using it to mark the date, location, and origin of the workshop as a way to keep all the iterations organized. Obviously, as the facilitator, it would make the most sense for you to retain the zines participants are creating; many senior citizens find it challenging to recall where they placed a single piece of paper from last week. To this end, it is practical to keep all of the zines, finished and unfinished, in the same manila folder. Subsequent workshops begin by introducing the zines you worked on last week. This gives your senior citizens an added boost of confidence in their abilities as zinesters by allowing them to "finish" their zines from last week--or start a new one.

Art by Crystal Burgoyne, 2005
Civil Liberties from Patriot Memory Game
Mixed Media
4"x5"x1/8"

Remembering Consciousness is Power: Working to Center Academic Library Outreach in the Service of Social Justice, Asian and Pacific Islander American Ethnic Visibility, and Coalition-Building

Melissa Cardenas-Dow
Judy Lee

Introduction

After numerous conversations between the authors on a number of topics, including being APIA (Asian Pacific Islander American) information professionals in a predominantly white profession and workplaces with varying and fluctuating degrees of supportiveness, we decided to write down our discussions. The result is this chapter, highly edited for the purposes of clarity and coherence, in which we take readers through various, interconnected themes of socially responsible and responsive library and information work and provide an autoethnographic, co-constructed view from our professional and personal positions. The idea for this work started with casual conversations the authors had been having off and on through a period of years. Around the time of the National Diversity in Libraries Conference held at the University of California, Los Angeles in 2016 (NDLC), our conversations became more frequent and coalesced into the themes of APIA information professionals, social justice work, visibility, institutional and community needs, and building relationships. We continued with observations while we attended the Joint Conference on Librarians of Color in Albuquerque in 2018 (JCLC). Thus, the idea for a chapter based on dialogue emerged.

Melissa Cardenas-Dow is a social sciences librarian at Sacramento State University, a campus in the California State University system. She has been working in libraries and library professional associations since 2009. She has also been involved in many diversity initiatives through the American Library Association's Office for Diversity, Literacy, and Outreach Services, working to infuse diversity and social justice throughout the Association and the library professions. She is currently an ALA Councilor-at-Large and a co-chair of the ALA Equity, Diversity and Inclusion Implementation Working Group.

Working in libraries since 1977, Judy Lee is currently the University Programs Teaching Librarian at the University of California, Riverside. Prior to the recent reorganization, she was a reference and instruction librarian with selection responsibilities for Asian American Studies and Women's Studies. In the first half of her career at UC Riverside, Judy participated in campus committees related to diversity and inclusion (affirmative action, women, Asian and Pacific Islander affairs). Over the last decade her diversity and inclusion activities branched out into the community: grassroots historic preservation (Chinese American and Japanese American); Multicultural Council (museum); Day of Inclusion programs; Asian American Walking Tours; etc.

Autoethnographic Analysis and Co-Created Narratives: Remembering Consciousness is Power

Inspired by the chapter offered by Bishop and Moffat (2016) in *Librarians With Spines, Volume 1*, we opted to structure this chapter as a dialogue--an interactive interview we conduct with each other. Following Bishop and Moffat, we assert that "social and cultural phenomena are both individually and collectively experienced" (p. 9), that our experiences of our world are simultaneously unique, individual and typical, as well as shared. We are cognizant of our participation in social systems, cultural institutions, and collectives that shape our understanding of our professional work, which in turn shape our personal perceptions. Our personal perceptions also shape our understanding of our professional work, as well as our participation in our selected social and cultural structures. And round and round it goes.

Ellis, Adams and Bochner (2011) write, "autoethnography is both process and product." They assert that autoethnographers "must use personal experience to illustrate facets of cultural experience, and, in so doing, make characteristics of a culture familiar for insiders and outsiders." While we do not claim cultural expertise, we do claim that our making sense of our circumstances as APIA women in the library and information profession illuminates particular aspects of library culture that resonates with many.

This chapter represents a longstanding conversation between the authors that has transpired over years. Our exchanges of ideas started at various reference desk shift changes when we both worked at the University of California Riverside Library, continued at the National Diversity in Libraries Conference (UCLA, 2016), the Joint Conference on Librarians of Color (Albuquerque, 2018), and in person, via Zoom, and email. Our conversation focuses on three themes: strengthening social justice in academic library outreach work, visibility among APIA librarians, and bridging institutional needs with community needs.

Judy Lee (JL): Thanks, Melissa, for pointing me to the National Diversity in Libraries Conference (NDLC, 2016) and encouraging me to sign up early for the Joint Conference on Librarians of Color (JCLC, 2018). I found the experiences rewarding and rejuvenating to be among librarians sharing their professional experiences and personal stories in a safe environment. It is always useful to hear what is going on at different places and being in such a setting is a bit different than hearing or reading about it. The conferences were havens for connecting with others and promoted learning, understanding, and kinship recognition. Anyone who has experienced a sense of personal or cultural isolation in a work-setting populated by those from a larger, more dominant culture would have appreciated attending the conferences, finding kindred spirits, and really knowing that one was not "alone."

Attending the conferences led to questions about myself and my professional career: my work and service for the library's patrons and the institution that employs me, and how the intersectionality of my experiences and attributes contribute to the work that I do, whether it be in the professional realm or in my various selected communities. I suspect that when we are dashing from one thing to another, too often in quick succession, this sort of reflection does not get its just due because of the time and effort required. Still, reflection is necessary.

I think that intersectionality brings a richness to our library work and adds to the success of the library organization. We are the sum of our attributes and experiences, each one experiencing different stages of development at any given point in time. In that sense, intersectionality brings a multidimensionality to our existence. That makes us all unique beings. It is too easy to forget that realization in our day-to-day encounters with others, and that realization also includes how we perceive ourselves. There are times that I am in awe of the connections, interrelationships, and communications that run in tandem, sequentially, or as a result of one another.

Melissa Cardenas-Dow (MCD): Thanks, Judy. Speaking of NDLC and JCLC, I agree they were wonderful, eye-opening experiences. I, too, ended up having questions about my personal and professional work, my roles in these different contextual realms, and the intersections of each. One large takeaway I had from both conferences is the huge significance of our origins, and how we make sense of life and the world through this lens. It's so important yet so often overlooked. Let's take some time to talk about this for a bit--both our professional and personal origins.

I'll start. I identify as a first-generation immigrant, right alongside my parents. They came to the United States in the early '80s from the Philippines. As I am sure you know, the Philippines was (or is) a colony of the United States. The ideal and idea of America was very prominent in mine and my parents' lives. I came to the United States with ideas and mental models that I've come to more deeply understand are inextricably linked to the history of Filipinos as a colonized people and the Philippines as an occupied land. I say "more deeply" because I do think Filipinos in the Philippines are very conscious of our colonial history and what we had come to call "colonial mentality." But for me, coming to the United States created greater intricacies to this awareness.

Professionally, I came to academic librarianship, as many do, as a second career. I didn't dream of becoming a librarian. I was a stay-at-home mother before I returned to school to study librarianship. Before that, I wanted to be a cultural studies scholar. As an undergraduate at San Francisco State University, I became very taken with Marxism, subaltern and postcolonial studies, and what was, at the time, the postmodern turn in cultural anthropology. My scholarly awareness was born in the late 1990s, when reflexivity and co-constructed narratives were huge in cultural anthropology. Combined with my time with teacher education and critical pedagogy courses before library school at San Jose State University, I can now see that my path to thinking, writing, and working about the junctions of information, diversity, and social justice had been set a long time ago.

I have brought all of these things with me, the personal and the professional, to my work in academic librarianship. In addition, I am very much aware of the perceptions my coworkers have of me and the pressure to perform in manners that are within expectations, however stereotypical, of female APIA workers. Fast forward to today, when I am now married to a white Midwesterner, with two mixed race children, employed as a Social Sciences Librarian at Sacramento State University, a public institution of higher education, with subject responsibilities in Psychology, Ethnic Studies, Family & Consumer Sciences, and Women's Studies.

My personal and professional interests can't help but be interwoven.

I'm still figuring a lot of things out, particularly how my personal history and experiences leave indelible marks on my professional work as an academic librarian, subject specialist, information literacy instructor, and scholar.

What about you, Judy? What contexts do you find yourself and your work operating within?

JL: Interesting, Melissa. The more we know about each other, the better understanding we have. And that can be critical to building trust and building a team in a close professional work environment. It can add another layer to what it means to be collegial.

My story varies a bit from yours, and, as with many immigration stories, there is kinship. I self-identify as a second-generation Chinese American whose father and grandfather were "paper sons."[1] Earlier, my mother had told me that I had "great great grandfathers" on both sides of the family who came to the United States to work on the railroads. I never found out if they were among the fortunate few who returned to China, or if they were among those who were never able to return, leaving behind family in the village. I grew up learning English when I went to school, although there may have been some beginnings of it at home -- I can't remember! The Chinese I learned was a dialect of Cantonese, the Toisan dialect, spoken by so many of the first wave of Chinese immigrants, like those who came to work on the railroads. Nowadays, hearing Toisan is not as common as hearing the standard Cantonese. As I was growing up, I was made aware that it was a dialect spoken by poorer, more rustic folk. I definitely am not fluent in it. I'm a baby boomer, married to a sansei, or third generation, Japanese American baby boomer. We have two adult-age children, a son and a daughter. Both of my parents

---

1 "Paper sons" (and, though rarer, "paper daughters") for Chinese and Chinese Americans refers to a specific illegal immigration phenomenon in response to the restrictive 1882 Chinese Exclusion Act and its successors. Those immigrants who were born in the United States (and their offspring) were allowed entry/re-entry to the country. The 1906 earthquake in San Francisco destroyed public birth documents that had been used as proof for legitimate entry. This set up a wave of pseudo-documents and claims that were sold (hence, "paper sons") to those seeking entry into the US. This meant constructing different identities and oftentimes changes of names, backgrounds, and villages. Elaborate coaching books were often part of the sale. They were studied to combat the minutely detailed questions that were asked at the immigration stations. Many families adopted the paper name in English while understanding that their Chinese names were different. For a discussion of paper sons, see pp. 84-90 in Angel Island... (Lee, E. and Yung, J., 2010) and this Los Angeles Times article about the family of a paper son (Ni, C., 2010). For an especially personal and poignant example of "paper daughters," please see Felicia Lowe's 2015 documentary film Chinese Couplets.

were immigrants while I and my brothers were born in California and were the first in our family to attend college. I was told to blend in, not make waves, and listen carefully to the teacher.

I went to library school directly out of college, having settled on the undergraduate Applied Behavioral Science major at UC Davis, which provided me a structure to express an interest in library science without having to write up and apply for an individual major. I supplemented the major program with self-initiated internships in a public library, the reference department of an academic library, and the California State Library setting. I was already working as a student assistant in Reserves on campus. My end project was creating a user's handbook to a specialized library, a new non-affiliated library within an academic unit for my last internship on campus. Although I think my path to librarianship made sense, I envy Gary Colmenar's path from an Ethnic Studies undergraduate major into library work, especially with the grounding he had with directed disciplinary study which he could apply to his career and collecting responsibilities (Colmenar, 2018).

I got my library degree from UC Berkeley when it still had an ALA-accredited curriculum. I admired the students in the program who came from another career (the more knowledge the better for libraries, right?) and wondered if I had what was required to become a successful librarian. I suspect that "imposter syndrome" and the worries that accompany it were present as early as library school even though I didn't realize it or understood what it was at the time. My first professional job was among four new positions at the University of Kansas. It was very different moving from a more diverse California population to the middle of the country where international students taking ESL would say to me that they appreciated my "excellent" English. Apparently my English was clear enough that they could understand me. I suppose my California "accent" was easier on their ears than the Midwestern twang of the region.

After a couple of years, I returned to California where I've since worked for the Riverside campus of the University of California system (UCR). One day I was on campus and wondered why things felt "different" and more comfortable. It dawned on me as I looked around, that there were more faces on campus that looked like mine. My professional work followed a standard path in reference, instruction, and collection development (primarily Asian American Studies and Women's Studies, a department which later changed to Gender and Sexuality

Studies). Unlike you, Melissa, I didn't consider social justice issues in a scholarly manner or within the context of libraries, academic disciplines, and society, although in my career at UCR I worked on campus affirmative action and Asian and Pacific Islander American advisory committees, as well as helped to establish the Chancellor's Advisory Committee on the Status of Women, including serving as one of its chairs.

My "awareness" of the intersectionality in my life began to focus around 10 years ago when I became involved in a local grassroots effort concerning Riverside's Chinatown (Cardenas-Dow, 2013). The work conducted and networks established on the community level and within the university context were intertwined and complimentary, which I find still true to this day. Practice in one setting guided and influenced the practice in the other.

For example, I had been asked to speak to various UC Riverside classes about the Save Our Chinatown Committee experience, a local grassroots effort to save from development a historic archaeological site with four levels of recognized landmark status (city, county, state, and national). When I was a guest presenter in the Introduction to Asian American Studies class, the faculty member also pointed out that I was a librarian and that those who might need assistance with their papers, should go to the library to ask for my help. When the Honors Program initially offered their seminar on "Engaging Riverside" I was asked to serve as one of two guest speakers for the segment covering Cultural Heritage in Riverside. That connection proved to be useful when my department was later reorganized and I became the University Programs Teaching Librarian. Honors was one of my constituent groups and the faculty member leading the "Engaging Riverside" course was the head of the Honors Program. We are now discussing the role the library might play in a revised Honors program course taken the year before the capstone project.

Intersectionality flows the other way as well. One of my community activities has been as a co-organizer and tour guide for the Riverside Asian American Walking Tours (RAAW Tours), where I always introduce myself as a librarian with UC Riverside. During the tour for the 2018 Asian Pacific Islander American Heritage Month, one of our tour stops was the assembly point where the Japanese Americans gathered to depart from Riverside by bus to the Assembly Centers. I pointed out that the UCR Library had in its Special Collections and University Archives the father and son diaries of Toranosuke Fujimoto (aka George, Senior) and George Fujimoto, Junior. People could go to the library and view the actual diaries; Toranosuke wrote in Japanese, George, Jr. wrote in English. Not only were tour participants able to look at the diaries themselves at the library, they would now be able to view digitized versions online from home. The Library's new Digitization Program had made it a priority to scan this set of diaries as one of its early projects, making them available just that year through the gateway to digital collections, Calisphere. I brought printed pages of the scans on Calisphere for the tour participants to view, including entries for the date the family left Riverside and later, when George Jr. returned to Riverside after serving his WWII stint in the Army. I was able to point out resources at the UCR Library and from online resources that touch local history in a community setting activity.

Intersectionality and Strengthening a Social Justice Ethos in Academic Library Outreach Programming

JL: Speaking of intersectionality, our experiences inform our practice and vice versa when our workplace selves coincide or interact with our personal selves and our community selves.

The specific details within each area will vary and be unique to each of us, as well as the numbers and types of areas. Our attributes will influence and provide an overlay to each component of our lives such as personality, age, gender, sexuality, family upbringing, cultural history, experience, and practices, and how far removed we might be from our family's immigrant generation. Other filters can include technology such as social media, and preferred communication or interaction styles, such as Grant's dichotomy of "takers," "matchers," and "givers" (Grant, 2013).

Specifically within our work environment, support for various projects that are relevant in the other arenas in our lives can have a significant impact on those projects and the personal integration of those components in our lives. It has influence on what we as individuals choose to do on our own time, what we do as professionals, and how those sectors cross over and interact. Sometimes these intersections can present conundrums or challenges, such as an individual's communications through social media representing a point of view in one arena that might come in conflict with or be problematic for another arena (such as a librarian's day job in an organization with public or government funding versus one's "other life" in another sector, such as being a publisher or member of an activist or community grassroots organization).

Boolean Who We Are

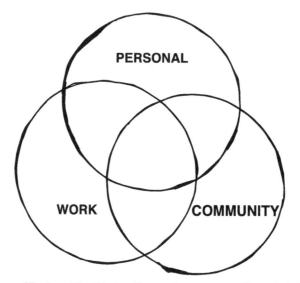

In the Venn diagram of Boolean Who We Are, Personal = our personal lives, including our perception of self and the factors that affect it; Work = our work and professional lives (e.g., environment, situations, issues, projects, etc.); and Community = the various defined communities to which we belong or which we serve.

MCD: That Venn diagram you've illustrated makes a tremendous amount of sense to me, Judy. It illustrates how integral the connections are between the different realms of our lives, how we can tap into one in order to enhance the other aspects.

I can see many applications to this. Just thinking about my own relationships at this stage in my life. A lot of them are deeply personal friendships with professional colleagues. We often help each other out by suggesting opportunities, providing feedback, and lending a shoulder, an ear, or hug. I often find myself looking for a similarly personal way of interacting with others from organizations and institutions. I don't know if it's realistic to have such an expectation. But in my mind attempting to put people first, human relationships first, is what I've come to expect. And I think this strengthens a social justice perspective, especially in outreach functions, when we're attempting to convince others to lend us trust, convincing them that we are worthy of being trusted.

Just to add some more dimension to this idea of intersectionality, I do think it is important to consider who we are within the landscape of the institution or organization we work within. In a different sort of illustration, I had co-authored an article on collaboration and the different things it could mean, especially from the position of an ethnic and gendered minority. I co-wrote the article with a dear friend and colleague, Linda Ueki Absher, and it's called "Collaborative Librarianship: A Minority Opinion" (Absher & Cardenas-Dow, 2016). In the article, we write about the issue of choice in the process of collaborating and how choice is often framed as a rational agreement that we enter into. The reality, however, tends to be more complicated--oftentimes involving a lack of choice since cooperation and collaboration can be a matter of survival.

One line from the article that I am especially proud of is: "Life in the margins is the lens through which we see our existence..." (p. 163). I feel this keenly. Most times, I have to suppress my thoughts and feelings, which come from the margins of American society, in order to maintain my professional position and the semblance of work success and status within my institution.

But this perspective of living life on the margins is the primary lens that I use when connecting and working with students and community members of color. Really, I think this can be as simple as having a human or personal demeanor. Sometimes I don't understand why an impersonal stance is equated with professionalism or good service or good customer relations. I think most people, especially those of us who crave and are glad to interact with other human beings, are looking for ways to work through an institution's policies with some warmth and connection from staff representing the organization. I do think we're strengthening the social justice ethos in an organization when we demonstrate person-to-person care and camaraderie in all services and programs, not just outreach activities.

JL: About that social justice ethos... Not long ago, I was again going over Lankes' introduction in his book The Atlas of New Librarianship (2011) and thought about the idea of libraries as places of neutrality: "The mission of librarians is to improve society through facilitating knowledge creation in their communities" (p. 10, fig. 4).

In that introduction, Lankes states that "Any attempt by librarians to wrap ourselves in the rhetoric and attitudes of some mythic detached scholar misses the point of understanding... The quest of truth is often described not as a methodological description of facts but of discovery." He concludes: "Example after example show that discovery of knowledge carries an equal obligation to fight ignorance and act. Scholarship is activism, truth is teaching, and librarianship is radical change. One must be both right and righteous" (p. 4). The conclusion is powerful.

Is that a mandate, a calling, or both? Whatever that might mean, it does mean consistent, continuous, day-to-day effort on our parts and that we librarians must be in it "for the long haul." That means various sustained and sometimes incremental actions from implementing policies to advance inclusion (and providing the examples to carry them out as well as meaningful measurements to illustrate progress), to working on structures of our knowledge base (e.g., subject headings or applications of thesaurus terms and less biased interpretations in the fields used), to instruction in and out of the classroom (from relevant relational examples, to acknowledgements of the various learning styles of our populations, to utilizing various technologies for learner engagement -- or choosing not to use them)[2]. On a personal note, I find that whenever I include some of my community work as examples and anecdotes during my instruction sessions, interest seems to perk up and several students have expressed interest by inquiring about them after the sessions.

I think part of this mandate or professional calling includes taking care of ourselves as well as taking care of others. Yes, Melissa, to return to one of your points, our relationships and human interactions are central to our professional, community, and professional lives.

---

2 One example of utilizing learning styles for APIA student populations can be found in Lee, H. (2016). Teaching Asianly, learning critically: A contextualized pedagogy to teach Asian American students in the US public schools. International Journal of Education and Social Sciences, 3(9), 1-7.

Enhancing the Visibility of Asian American Librarians

JL: At UC Riverside where I work, our undergraduate population reflects[3] a fairly high level of diversity. Attention and support are directed so our students of color can attain their degrees in a timely fashion. The numbers at the graduate student level, faculty, staff, and general senior management positions do not quite reflect the kinds of numbers achieved at the undergraduate level but they are slowly improving. Remember when I mentioned earlier about feeling more comfortable on campus? After that observation, I felt like I was somehow contributing to the

> Scholarship is activism, truth is teaching, and librarianship is radical change. One must be both right and righteous.

campus effort as a librarian of color when I worked with individuals or groups of students or spoke to them in classes or at orientations--whether they were APIA, African American, Chicana/o, or Native American students. It was as much a sense of my belonging on campus as it was of having students of color feel included on campus. I think I was also hoping to speak to them as a librarian who happened to be a librarian of color, and that this occurrence was a normal, rather than unusual circumstance.

MCD: That's a really great way of framing visibility and representation on campus, Judy. Among undergraduates, I do think we are pretty similar in that Sacramento

---

3 From the Fall 2017 statistics, 11.5% identify as white students. (Native American: 0.1%, International: 2.9%, African American: 3.5%, Multi-Racial: 5.7%, Asian: 33.8%, Hispanic/Latino: 41.3%)

Graduate student statistics are a little different: https://diversity.ucr.edu/statistics/studentstat.html

The campus has received numerous diversity awards, the latest one being named one of INSIGHT into Diversity's 2018 Higher Education Excellence in Diversity (HEED). It was the lone UC campus listed. (This publication is the oldest and largest diversity publication in higher education.) https://news.ucr.edu/articles/2018/08/29/uc-riverside-receives-diversity-award

State University's campus demographics has great representation among students of color. Similar to your institution, the levels we enjoy among undergraduate students are not reflected among our graduate students, our faculty, staff, and senior administration. Similar to you, my level of comfort on my campus has to do with the representation of people of color[4] among our undergraduate student population. Of course, I do tend to focus my work and professional attention on undergrads, so there is that.

There is also the question of enhancing visibility for APIA librarians on campus, one that we had been discussing for a while now. Care to speak more on this topic?

JL: What does it mean to enhance the visibility of APIA librarians? How do we achieve visibility? Do we need to be at center stage, lead causes, or make a significant impact? That is entirely possible, but I think it is *not* the only way to enhance our visibility. It took me awhile to come to this realization. Perhaps I felt guilty about *not* being the person out front as a take-charge leader for diversity and social justice efforts, or that in not being obviously out there that I had failed to contribute to the overall effort. Personality types and comfort levels are important factors to take into consideration. APIA librarians need not always be in front to achieve change. I now think that with every project, committee assignment, or task we undertake, including speaking at group events, we APIA librarians can model the behavior we want to see, individually or as part of a group, such as a committee or organization. This could transpire within a setting of mostly APIAs, a setting of diverse populations, or even if we address populations different than ourselves. Our consistent daily interactions can incrementally affect our visibility and potentially change stereotypes. I hope that these consistent incremental occurrences move the perception of those behaviors from something "different" and noticeable into the realm of what is "normal" and not required to "stand out." Surely these considerations are not felt only by APIA librarians. I wonder how many librarians of color also share these thoughts and experiences.

---

4 Sacramento State University publishes its undergraduate student demographics on its website: https://www.csus.edu/about/ For more detailed information, such as the differences between undergraduate and graduate student demographics: https://www.csus.edu/oir/datacenter/studentspecialreports/longtermtrends/ethnicity.html and the faculty and staff profiles: https://www.csus.edu/oir/datacenter/universityfactbook/SEC%201%20-%20Faculty-Staff.pdf, please see the webpages of the Sacramento State University's Office of Institutional Research, Planning & Effectiveness (https://www.csus.edu/oir/).

Another aspect of visibility is when we APIA librarians are seen working with other people of color (PoC). Working with other PoC for a common goal enhances our visibility in other ways, and can enhance social justice goals and projects, serving as a visible reinforcement within our communities. Building coalitions enhances our work and increases our networking and audience communication.

MCD: I agree with this tremendously. I do think that we need to articulate clearly what we mean by visibility,not just the various ways we can work to enhance it. One way as you've stated, is definitely the normalization of APIA librarians and the work we do. Another is by working with other ethnic minorities and marginalized groups on campus. This not only frames our visibility as potential partners, but friends and allies as well.

Then there is the other side of visibility, which we'd talked about previously in other contexts. That side that requires us to address stereotypes directly and which affects the dynamics of our visibility and invisibility, as well as our marginalization (and lack of).

JL: Yes, this myth and stereotype can be either boon or bane, depending on the circumstances. Of the racial-ethnic groups in the United States as a media stereotype, APIAs tend to be portrayed negatively, and although some positive stereotypes have emerged to match changing societal circumstances, the longstanding stereotypes have remained stable and recognizable to the populace.[5]

It would be interesting to find out how these stereotypes might affect the perceptions of people of color and what roles those stereotypes play in ethnic and interracial communication and behaviors. While APIAs are perceived as most likely to achieve academic success, they are also more likely to be perceived as nerds, most likely to be left out, and the least likely to have friendships initiated with them (Zhang, 2010). Of course, one would hope that people in an academic environment might be more aware of these issues and would approach interactions with fewer preconceived notions, but that is not always the case.

---

5 Some examples of these stereotypes of APIAs are: the model minority (academically overachieving, good at math, does not question or rock the boat, non-threatening), apolitical, asexual, not creative or artistic. See Zhang (2010) for greater detail.

Without doubt, the model minority myth affects the APIA librarian (how we view ourselves and what we perceive how others view us), the library patrons (be they APIAs or not), and library colleagues and co-workers (APIA or not, employees within the library or from the academic institution). This mythic stereotype follows APIA librarians and can thrust us into the limelight, marginalize us, or place us somewhere in between. It is part of us and impacts our visibility as well as our *invisibility*.

The myth affects our work environment and how well we perform our jobs. What projects do we select or are selected for us? Are we a vital part of the team, or are we token members? Do we chair committees? Are we steered toward or away from certain kinds of positions, certain kinds of work, particular duties or tasks? Would we ourselves shy away from specific work or committees because we do not wish to be typecast as "the diversity person"? On another note, would we APIA librarians take note of the myth and modify our behaviors in a given situation based on what we consider the behaviors or reactions of others in that situation might be? How much do we modify our behaviors given our own assumptions of the situation?

I have had the experience where a colleague in a couple of community organizations, who is also a woman of color but not APIA, recommended -- well, "pushed" -- me forward as a speaker, moderator, or emcee because she felt that my "Asian face" should be "out there" in the public to represent that part of the community, and also to be seen as part of this particular organization from that represented community. There are times when I appreciate why this colleague did this, but there are also times when I actually got a bit annoyed at being placed in the position as the "one" who represents the APIA community or the "one" representing the organization and providing legitimacy for the organization because I am of a particular community. This phenomenon also occurs for various committee memberships in the work setting, be it in the library or on campus. Intersectionalities in the web of pressures and negative stressors abound here, don't they?

Just how "representative" am I and how appropriate, fair, or burdensome does that "responsibility" feel? How much am I selected for my accident of birth rather than for my skills? Then the question crops up: would I have been selected for my skills alone? Of course, there are situations when the ethnicity factor is the *only* way one would be selected to serve and those situations are defined by representative membership. Occasionally that ethnicity factor could work against a person -- as in the position that we already have "enough" representation from this or that group on the committee.

MCD: Yes, I often find myself thinking about this tension as well.

JL: I mean, do we engage in self-censorship? Are there times when we might normally speak up or act, but consciously decide not to respond? Should we choose not to respond at that time, how do we feel about that action? How does that self-censorship affect us, the people around us, and our work?

With the "Asian face" example in community organizations, I may be discomforted at finding myself in that position yet again and feel contrary about accepting that role at that time. I might occasionally refuse the role others want me to take, a role I might otherwise accept at another moment in time. I'm not quite sure how to deal with those conflicting feelings, just as I am not sure how others around me would react or feel when I am "acting contrary."

The myth can also provide opportunities to counter stereotypes. Can we use it to our advantage, to perform in the moment, an educational jujitsu movement which might affect the perceptions others may have of us? Simply doing our jobs or the tasks of daily life can steadily and incrementally build or affect perceptions that others have of us. How aware are we when those moments present themselves? How much of a conscious effort would that take on our parts? How much of that effort or attempt can be embedded "automatically" within our professional selves and our personal ones? What actions might one take beyond what is defined as one's job? When do we decide to take those actions that move APIA librarians toward the greater good of enhancing our visibility? Do we recognize what the tipping point may be in order for us to do so? Is it okay not to "step up to the plate" every time? And why?

I think our energy levels fluctuate and stepping up or down is part of the self-care that we need to recognize for ourselves. We can't do everything. We can't do it all the time. For me, the "answer" is yes, it's okay not to step up to the plate every time. By giving ourselves permission, we can then think about being selective, being strategic about when those moments to step up are. It can be one method of self-care that we can provide for ourselves. Of course, taking this approach might mean conducting some inner discussions with ourselves and making peace with such topics as "self-care," consistency, and core values.

If we have mentors or colleagues around who are facing the same situation, perhaps we can work with each other to lighten that load, or to share strategy of how to handle a situation together, or even if one person needs to pass that particular time, how to go about dealing with the situation.

MCD: I have to say I often ask myself if I ought to hang back. I am often encouraged by people to do so for practical reasons of personal capacity and being professionally strategic. But I've also noticed that those who encourage me to continue to step up seem to have a fuller grasp of the needed work for advocating for marginalized people.

Other factors they also encourage me to consider are those of privilege and whiteness. APIAs, I think, are at times considered to be "honorary whites." Privileges that accompany the model minority stereotype may emanate from that honorary orientation, ideas about social position and socioeconomic class, or ascription to what it means to be a "professional" or a "professional librarian." Despite these perceptions, APIAs are marginalized even though we are not read as such. I've seen this from some comments and behaviors of other people of color. I've often been complemented by other people of color for my good grasp of the English language. I've also been expected to perform well academically by individuals from communities of color.

Also, some APIAs support aspects of whiteness and privilege. We have to come to terms with elements in our community that claim the model minority idea, proudly wear it and use it, whatever the reason. These conditions can complicate our APIA place in the social justice work we do, in allyship, or in bridging coalitions in our communities. In the realm of higher education, I recently saw this play out in the news about the effort to legally end affirmative action in Harvard University's admissions policies.[66]

In many ways, APIA librarians can (and should) claim the work of cultural memory; in many ways, we do work to unearth memory and making them relevant

---

6 See Wermund, B. (2018, October 14). GOP courts Asian-Americans with drive to end affirmative action. Politico. Retrieved from https://www.politico.com/story/2018/10/14/asian-americans-affirmative-action-898521

again. Archives and libraries do quite a bit to preserve, including the provision of context for prior work in different fields, highlighting of cultural memory. Ethnic Studies librarians bring examples to the fore to inform others. Ironically, positions and academic studies that aim to facilitate, preserve, and uncover work for and within marginalized communities can be considered dead-end areas for professionals of color. Jobs such as subject specialists and liaisons, and collection development strategists in area studies and ethnic studies could end up hindering rather than helping advancement in the workplace hierarchy. But it's needed work!

JL: That is so true! At the same time, we APIAs need to recognize our privileges as well as our marginalization as we negotiate our relationships with white people and other people of color, in both higher education settings and the larger society. That's when it becomes important to be open with, as well as understanding and supportive of others. Transparency is important; we need to acknowledge our "not really knowing" the experience of others with a willingness and honest attempt to look from a view other than our own. I know that's not always easy to take on, especially if we have not yet resolved the idea of privilege for ourselves, considered how much privilege we actually experience and "own," and have examined what we do with it.

Bridging Institutional Needs with Community Needs

MCD: And while we APIAs recognize and feel the needs of our communities, we also know and feel the needs of our places of work, the institutions and organizations that employ us. While these various needs can clash and conflict, they can also be bridged. What do you think about bridging institutional needs with community needs, Judy?

JL: There are many approaches to develop this bridge. One way is to collaborate with other groups to build coalitions and mutually beneficial programs and projects.

Recently, I was directly involved with planning Riverside's 8th annual

Day of Inclusion event as a member of the Multicultural Council for the Riverside Metropolitan Museum. In short, December 17th was set aside in 2009 by a California Assembly Concurrent Resolution (ACR 76) to be recognized as the Day of Inclusion, the day in 1943 when the Magnuson Act was signed in Congress and finally repealed the infamous Chinese Exclusion Act of 1882. However, instead of focusing on the negative exclusionary aspects, the day focuses on celebrating inclusion and the current diversity of California's cultures.

The 2018 program celebrated the 75th anniversary of the Magnuson Act with the theme "Memories of Migration: Diverse Journeys." Karthick Ramakrishnan from UC Riverside was the keynote speaker. His research group and other organizations had prepared the report *State of Immigrants in the Inland Empire* which significantly, contained local regional information as well as sidebar profiles of individual immigrants. Learning about the facts of local immigration adds to our history and rich cultural heritage of the region. It adds to the community's public knowledge and understanding about itself. This annual program also coincides with the Mayor's and City Council's *Annual Reaffirmation of Building a More Inclusive Riverside Community Statement* as well as their annual proclamation recognizing and celebrating the Day of Inclusion in Riverside.

This year the Multicultural Council encouraged and recommended this theme to others for its potential offshoots and community involvement in offering similar programs for the coming year. In the past, various groups supported the Day of Inclusion event as a co-sponsor and/or having a community group table at the event (e.g., the Riverside Japanese American Citizens League [JACL], the Save Our Chinatown Committee, the Riverside Museum Associates). This year, community group involvement expanded (e.g., Inlandia Institute, the Riverside Art Museum, and some departments at UC Riverside). Already, the Inlandia Institute planned writing workshops in 2018 and the Riverside Art Museum's exhibit in the latter part of 2018 dovetailed with the theme. The event venue was at a community center located in the city's ward that included the university as well as two major communities of color and garnered support from the Ward Councilmember.

Community benefits include a program that supports the educational mission of the Riverside Metropolitan Museum, increasing local awareness of the cultural histories of its diverse communities, and promoting various community groups to work separately or together on a common theme. The benefit to the university is recognition of the relevant research conducted by the university and its research partners. As a public institution, educating the public about this kind of work and its relevance to the local community is important to highlight and establish university-community ties and relationships as well as providing additional justification for the university and its work.

MCD: That's a great example of finding mutual aims and collaboration between communities and institutions, Judy! I can't agree more. Though work to advance knowledge is important, I also think that work that develops goodwill and enhances the relationships between institutions of higher learning and the communities that surround and support them are also extremely necessary. As you say, it justifies the work of the public university and by extension, our work as academic librarians in the public university.

One question about this that we had previously discussed is how should such personal and professional investments in individual people's time and

> People are important.
> Engage them. Find allies
> and likeminded people.
> Don't go it alone.

energy be acknowledged? Faculty members like Dr. Ramakrishnan, I think, get some sort of acknowledgement through the academic review process. But do the librarians of color like you, get similar acknowledgement? Whether you seek it or not? Sometimes I think library organizations, and by extension many library professionals, emphasize results and products, such as how many bodies attend a program or used a service. We forget that work focused on relationship-building is just as, if not more, crucial to the success of any outreach endeavor. Lack of trust may be a significant factor to why bodies don't attend a program or use a service.

Practice: a Combination of Thought and Action

MCD: So what to do? How do we translate all these perspectives and mental concepts into our actions and behaviors? Especially of those of us who are employed in a public university as academic librarians? That's the huge crux of the problem we all face, right?

Let's start with the piece of advice that says, "People are important. Engage them. Find allies and likeminded people. Don't go it alone."

> Identify what matters to
> you. Identify and define
> your communities and
> determine what matters
> to them.

JL: There are so many ways to recast or reframe that piece of advice! I think the recent article in *American Libraries* gave great pieces of advice along these lines. Miriam Tuliao (Yamaguchi, 2018) emphasized finding one's library "family." From the same article, Lisa Chow advised, "be vocal and visible."

This advice also stresses that library work is all about relationships: the one librarians have with their patrons and their patron communities, the one librarians have with their disciplines (be it the library profession or a disciplinary specialty within the library field -- like preservation -- or disciplinary selection responsibilities -- like ethnic studies -- or as some kind of "specialist" role -- e.g., the makerspace librarian), the ones librarians have with each other (be they personal networks or professional groups and associations), the ones librarians have with other professionals so that the library functions (be it the larger organization like the university for an academic library, the board that oversees library organizational work and activities, fundraising partners and donors, government agencies/officials/workers, or friends of the library, etc.). I strongly believe that relationships make the library work. Then there's the quality of those relationships that can make or break the opportunities for individual librarians and the library organization.

MCD: I agree these are great pieces of advice. Though they're easier said than done, they do need to be said and repeated every once in a while. Building relationships with others either through professional associations or workplace and community networks are necessary and are not optional matters.

I think being aware of the contexts within which you operate is also important. Along with the advice that places people above other concerns, I offer "Identify what matters to you. Identify and define your communities and determine what matters to them." I do think it is vital to acknowledge that what matters to the community is determined by the community members themselves, instead of being imposed from outside. Of course, there will be conflicts among community members and priorities and of course, not all concerns deemed by a group will matter in a similar way to those who are not members of the group.

I take this same attitude to my work in professional associations. For me, the professional associations I have been involved with are among the communities I think I am a part of. They help me reflect and do this internal work of thinking and identifying. This reflective practice then helps me with other community-based relationships and activities in my life. There may be other ways to develop identifications and ways to support a person's reflective practice.

Think relationally.

JL: Absolutely, Melissa! So glad that professional associations as part of your community works well for you! While I try to encourage the practice of seeking help and advice for my patrons, I confess that I did not always follow that advice for my own career path and regret that I did not make more of an effort to seek mentors or advice from APIA librarians. Something else that I've noticed is that although I might work with APIA colleagues in my own institution, our conversations do not necessarily gravitate toward diversity, equity, inclusion, or social justice issues. Therefore, I am glad to see networks such as APALA (Asian/Pacific American

Librarians Association) and CALA (Chinese American Librarians Association) that not only encourage such advice and collaboration, but also provide an active community for library professionals at all stages in their careers. If it is not easy to find an APIA mentor or co-discussant, perhaps adoption of a more reflective practice could help. A useful recent resource on reflective practice for librarians was published by ALA and is listed in our references (Reale, 2017).

While keeping a journal is a standard way for reflection, I find that one way I reflect is by adding "notes to self" -- my own observations about my instruction sessions, feedback or suggestions from the disciplinary course instructor, or considerations for next time in the entries where we keep our statistics. It seems to be a logical place for me to do that as I'm reviewing how the class went after the session. Sometimes this reflection could be time-consuming though, so it's not an approach for everyone, although one does not have to enter that information for every session. Just wanted to point it out as another possibility to consider.

> No matter how goal-oriented you are, a good chunk of your success depends on your peripheral vision.

MCD: Another thing that came up from our discussions is the idea of putting relational thinking in opposition to efficiency. In my mind, I had always thought of thinking relationally as having a human-centered approach--people are both the means and the ends--while efficiency tends to view human beings as resources that are often expendable and mere means to a desired end. So how about giving the advice of "Think relationally"?

In information literacy and instruction, we make every effort to teach using a learner-centered approach. What could (and would) happen in a management setting that takes an employee-centered approach? Employee as a human being with attached social circles, concerns and priorities? Business and management literature have long been advocating for shifting practice and thinking toward the people who work to make the business and its organizational operations function. What changes would we encounter in the library-as-workplace setting? In academic libraries?

JL: Yes, why not in libraries, too? Again, with the relationship building and thinking relationally in our "front-line practice," so to speak, can they also be applied successfully within the operational structure of a library? Also, how do various communities, like communities of color, utilize these and other concepts in building and organizing their communities? Can we learn something from other points of view for our work and organizations?

I suppose to a great extent, we have some of this happening already, so maybe it's just a matter of following the idea to its ends. Part of relational thinking and personnel management can involve issues of diversity, equity, and inclusion as well as social justice issues within the structure of the library organization and institution, and in the structure and services of the library to its patrons and clientele. We can choose to add those issues as filters to our relational styles. They permeate our lives and can add a consistency to our efforts.

What do you think of the idea of "No matter how goal-oriented you are, a good chunk of your success depends on your peripheral vision"? I got that from an article (Simmons, 2013) that discussed efficiency thinking and progressed to relational thinking (Komisar, 2001) and the power of relationships (Collins, 2001), which then led me to the quote attributed in the article to Grant, another bestselling author who was referred to earlier in our conversation (Grant, 2013).

MCD: I think it's great, but it does need some explanation. I'm sure the book gives it. By the way, more writing from the business/management/leadership realm!

JL: Yes! The comment illustrates relational thinking and the need for openness. Receptivity to ideas other than one's own is so very important. Situations may require us to take leaps of faith and find steps in reality, where we can locate and negotiate the handholds and footholds to take us through them.

MCD: I agree with that. In my own experience, opportunities don't always hit you head on. They come from the side and if you turn to look straight at them, they kind of disappear or move to the periphery yet again. This piece of advice tells me that there is a dynamic aspect to existence that makes receptivity and openness necessary. Making connections and anticipating relatedness of ideas, concepts, and people are an important part of making sense of most things. With this unpredictability comes a particularly humble approach to most things. And the realization that there's too much to know and to learn, that certitude is often contextual, contingent, and relational. And now we are back to relational thinking.

> You are enough.

JL: After NDLC in 2016 I ran into a blog post by Konrad Ng, who I had heard at one of the Asian and Pacific Islander American Historic Preservation Fora (APIAHiP). At that forum I was impressed by his insight and that he was heading up the Smithsonian Institution's Asian Pacific American Center. That he was also President Obama's brother-in-law was an added bonus. Writing about his experience at the Smithsonian in the blog post, I was struck by Ng's appreciation of small acts.

"Acts of kindness, of empathy, of generosity, of compromise, of recognition and the like, are the threads of civil society. These small acts amount to being able to see ourselves in one another, and recognizing that our future is shared." (Ng, 2016). This was recognized by social activist, philosopher, and feminist Grace Lee Boggs, who Ng quotes as having said, "[D]oing small things at the local level, like planting community gardens or looking out for our neighbors. That is how change takes place in living systems, not from above but from within, from many local actions occurring simultaneously." (Ng, 2016; Hollander, 2015). I like that: consistent, incremental steps that have an impact in and of themselves as well as impact from the acts taken together.

So, here's another piece to mull over: "Relish the possibilities and value of each act, big or small."

MCD: I really like that thought, especially since it has the potential to link our individual, personal acts to systemic and institutional changes. Like many others, I feel the pressure to act big and only count the big actions in service of social justice. Similarly, I often think of my foul-ups, even the miniscule ones, as monumental catastrophes. I'd like to think that relishing, appreciating, and valuing possibilities of big and small actions require us to gain some perspective on both our triumphs and failures.

It's very easy to be overwhelmed by the sheer weight and immensity of the problems we face: racism, misogyny, fear and rejection of anyone and anything that is foreign, impure, other. Not to mention the unintended negative consequences that often follow our well-intended acts. Refocusing on the minute possibilities, therefore, is necessary.

> Relish the possibilities
> and value of each act,
> big or small.

JL: I hear you about the pressure to count only the big actions and the tendency to magnify one's own missteps as a major catastrophe. Sometimes the only time we realize that a "little act" we do is not so little is when someone tells us how much that action meant to them. Perhaps we all need to remember to acknowledge these appreciations of those acts to others. That can add to the refocusing on the smaller possibilities, particularly when we feel overwhelmed by the larger issues.

Actually, Melissa, I'd like to return to a thought earlier in our conversation, and that is we do not have to make a big splash or be at center stage to have an impact; that we can have an impact by how we live our lives and carry on with our professional roles and responsibilities, that our impacts count. The thought ties into some of that self-care practice we should encourage and nurture. It touches upon the imposter syndrome issue.

And that is "You are enough."

No guilt. Do not "always" feel guilty about what you do not or cannot do (although some of us are not able to help ourselves). Not everyone can, or should, be ALA President.

Sandra Sajonas: "Don't be the 'Asian workhorse'...Be clear about your limits." (Yamaguchi, 2018). Sandra was warning about the trap of Asian Americans falling into the expectations of others that Asian Americans would not complain or the stereotype of Asian Americans shouldering a lot of work and responsibility. So, for those Asian Americans who do tend to take on a lot of work, the warning is to recognize reasonable limits and not to overload or always take on the burden (Yamaguchi, 2018).

I have a colleague with "Enough" tattooed as a reminder where she could easily find it.

MCD: On its face, I do like this. It supports the acts of relishing and valuing our well-intended efforts that we had discussed earlier. And it can serve the purpose of countering the messages we get from elsewhere that we have to constantly work on improving something about ourselves. For those of us who live in the margins, we receive the messages that we will never be enough however hard we try and however much we accomplish. In such a context, I get it and can welcome the message, and very much appreciate how it figures prominently into much needed self-care.

But I do have a "but." Even though I don't see myself as, to use your example, ALA President one day, I also viscerally feel the pull of work that needs to be done. And, yes, I derive great satisfaction on being that "Asian workhorse." It is extremely nice to be valued and appreciated, and such validation boosts my desire to continue working; I do admit however, that recognition isn't the primary motivating factor for me. The work motivates me. Being part of something larger than myself motivates me. When I think of being "enough," a small voice asks me what that is, what limits am I setting for myself, have they been created for and imposed upon me, and if such limits are temporary or permanent. Overloading is one thing. But it's quite another to decline an opportunity due to limits set by other circumstances and situations. Amidst such circumstances and situations, I do wonder where my own will or agency figures.

And since working for social justice involves pushing the limits of current social circumstances, situations, and states, I often encounter limits within myself that aren't easily applicable to the palatable idea of "I am enough." Internal conflicts between what I envision to be kinder and more just actions and my unexamined, bias-laden, knee-jerk reactions--these are things I think we all wrestle with. Examining this internal conflict, and remembering that consciousness is within our personal power, is important. We are all immersed in misogyny, racism, inequity, and xenophobia. These are the waters within which we fish swim and live. And many of us are only just becoming aware of the existence of the water that surrounds, sustains, makes, and defines us. The "enough" message, therefore, can easily slide into complacency, so I'd put an asterisk on that. I'm not saying that complacency follows the "enough" message. I'm just saying that taken to the message's ends, the potential is strong.

> You can be enough.

JL: Wow. I hadn't really thought about more than one way of interpreting "enough." As you rightly point out, there are many considerations that can apply to that concept depending on one's circumstances, experiences, personal vs. institutional standards, and intrinsic vs. extrinsic motivations. Your comments are examples of those questions and interpretations that many may work through in determining what "enough" means to them. Interpretation of a concept is also a **relational** act and "enough" defined for one is not always the same as "enough" defined by another.

When I proposed "enough" I was approaching it with the idea that many APIA professionals work hard and put such great effort into their jobs and the profession that it is easy for them (for us) to overextend and burn out. The added bind of being different, the "other," or from the margins can mean trying to prove oneself by being "better than the best"--that excellent rating held by the institutional work standard, whatever that particular definition may be. In this case I was also thinking of "enough" as part of self-care to guard against overextending ourselves to the point of burnout or breaking. Big issues can be overwhelming. We all need something, whether it be brakes, breaks, rest, or distractions to get through the overwhelming moments in order to carry on. So, yes, to your initial response in interpreting what I had meant.

In academia we both have seen and heard discussed review criteria that sounds like one has to "walk on water" in order to advance (to be considered "worthy"?) – hence, the ALA President example. (Also, statistically the chances any one person has of obtaining that particular position is not realistic! What is the definition of excellence that falls within reason? Whose definition of excellence is reasonable? What is achievable?)

Thank you for including the "but" comments. They are considerations that have added to my edification. (You just provided another example that **people are important; engage them**.)

> Consciousness is power.

Hopefully one's definition of "enough" will not become an excuse to stop or become complacent, although for some, it certainly will be. For some people, the intrinsic and extrinsic motivations become the same. For others, both exist with differences and both are important. For still others, one type is more important to achieve than the other. (I think about early career professionals, for example.) Some of our motivations and actions are more heavily weighted or impacted by the opinions of individuals we value, who may or may not be our evaluators at work. Certainly, we all need to determine what our personal aspirations, goals, and outcome satisfactions are, that which could be reasonable for each of us yet still be inspiring. Some of that value determination comes through conversations we have with ourselves, some through conversations we have with others. (Don't go it alone.)

I guess for some the advice is "**you are enough**." For others, it is "**you can be enough**." But there can be much more beyond those statements.

Thoughts, conversations, and ruminations are key to our conscious development, individually and collectively. And remember, consciousness is power.

Artwork by Shanalee Hampton
www.shanaleehampton.com

Speaking Out of Turn: Reflections from Behind the Reference Desk

Sheila Garcia
Erica Soto
Angelo Moreno
Nephtali Gomez

In late 2014, five paraprofessionals working in a library system in the Midwest met informally to brainstorm ways in which the a midwest library system could improve services to their local Latinx community. After a few meetings, it became clear that the mission was one their institution not only shared, but that directly aligned with the library's strategic plan. Shortly thereafter, their informal group became formalized as the Latinx Advisory Committee (LAC) of the public library.

The two years this committee was active were filled with highs and lows; while library administrators recognized the importance of their work for the community, their paraprofessional classification and lack of dedicated funding limited the scope of what they were able to accomplish. Nevertheless, after meeting with Latinx community leaders and forming relationships with local organizations to determine which services needed to be improved and expanded on, the LAC was able to complete several initiatives to meet the community's needs. These included the addition of an immigration services webpage to the library website, spearheading the translation of the library catalog to Spanish, the inclusion of Spanish language story times, and community outreach to the Latinx public, among other initiatives.

Four years after this first meeting, four of the five founding members-- Erica Soto, Angelo Moreno, Nephtali Gomez, and Sheila Garcia--met to reflect on their experiences as committee members. Their conversation was recorded, transcribed, and then edited to ensure that tone and other nuances from the audio were captured in the text. This conversation is meant to serve not only as a final debrief for LAC members, but also as a starting point to a wider conversation of advocating and organizing as paraprofessionals within a profession where delineated roles and rigid structure can stifle innovation and engagement.

Sheila: Thank you all for being here. Let's get started with a foundational question: what did or does the LAC mean to you?

Erica: The LAC meant and means community and connection. It means wanting to keep the Latinx population of our community informed and educated about the necessary resources available for their lives and families to thrive. It means being the face and ear for individuals who need help but maybe don't feel confidence in seeking higher knowledge. It means being responsible for helping our community grow. Unfortunately, the LAC also meant being disappointed in an institution that should have embraced our efforts more.

I don't want to sound like we're disgruntled. I just want to be genuine and informative so people can understand things [that happened] and the way we feel about it. Often ideas were not listened to or respected, especially with information professionals of color who were trying to reach communities that don't take advantage of libraries like they should because they haven't been able to make a strong connection with their local library. Whether it be through language difference, citizenship status, fear of sounding incompetent, and sometimes even fear of asking for help, these barriers are real and we were the faces and voices they could identify with that eased those barriers. I don't think the institution took into account that there was a passionate group of us ready, willing, and able to put our boots on the ground and serve, like they should have. Instead, we endured many unnecessary hurdles as if constantly needing to justify why our voices as Latinx professionals mattered for our community.

Sheila: Right. And you'll find that most information professionals of color face exactly the same things that we did. So we weren't necessarily the exception to the rule. I do think our experience was a unique one because we experienced it as a group rather than as individuals.

Angelo: Erica, you mentioned that there were unnecessary hurdles. Can you expand on that?

Erica: There were many little hurdles or things that felt wrong. We were not listened to or valued as much as we should have been.

For example, I experienced an uncomfortable situation with a former leader of the LAC. I took the liberty to create an agenda for one of our upcoming meetings. This bothered her so much, that instead of telling me that she had a problem with me creating the agenda, she went to my supervisor. He confronted me when I arrived for my shift the next day and basically said, "Stay in your place, don't overstep another librarian." I responded that all I did was create an agenda and was confused about why he came at me so harshly. He never visited our branch for anything, even as a supervisor, so I felt directly targeted.

I became extremely anxious about being reprimanded and confronted her face-to-face about it when I finally saw her. I asked her, "What was the point of that? You could have just emailed me and said, 'Hey Erica, I got it'." You know what I mean? Then at our meeting, we ended up using the very same agenda I was reprimanded for for creating. So, little things like that intentionally discouraged us, especially when we were treated unfairly and literally told, "No, this is your place." I felt powerless in that situation. That's what I mean by unnecessary hurdles. We just want to help--add our skills or input--but then we realize, "No, this is as far as we can go."

Sheila: I think to an extent, we faced two levels of barriers. One of them being that we were all primarily paraprofessionals, trying to get our voice heard among library professionals. And generally from what I've seen, paraprofessionals aren't perceived--I don't want to say on the same level--but, because library professionals have to get a Master's degree, they are believed to be capable and understanding of certain professional practices that paraprofessionals are not. So that's a very, very big overstatement, but there are little pieces of that type of thinking that I would see in how some people carried themselves every day. For example, not even trying to learn the name of the Pages because turnover is high.

The other level of barriers relates to trying to advocate for the community without the resources to truly understand the administrative structures in place at the library. There were ways that you had to and should have done things that weren't explicitly explained. Not knowing how to submit paperwork through the right channels within specific timeframes often prevented us from making the most of our capabilities. And while I know and understand why these structures are in place, a lack of transparency about the process led to this becoming a barrier rather than a process we could use to our advantage.

Nephtali: I definitely felt that, especially towards the end. Like, "Oh, you're supposed to be doing it this certain way." No one really told us. We had all these great ideas and were being constantly told "we can't do this" or "oh, you didn't turn it in on time" or "you didn't submit an application or a form for it." We were just shut down. Towards the end of our term, we were finally able to get better insight only after we met with a library administrator about next steps for the group. That was the time when Sheila and Erica left the library and of course me as a paraprofessional, I don't have the authority or power behind me to really continue with the committee.

Angelo: I don't know that story about the meeting with the library administrator...?

Sheila: When you left, Angelo, we didn't have anyone leading us. This library administrator met with us and told us that she was going to have each of us be part of different committees so that we could each have a say in different library departments. She added me to the Adult Programming Committee and then she added Erica to the Early Literacy Committee. Then she said Nephtali would work more closely with circulation administrators to figure out new outreach initiatives to the Latinx community. The idea was for us to then come back together and brainstorm new initiatives, but nothing was really set in place.

Erica: So instead of keeping us together as a group that could directly communicate with the Latinx community and still advise them, their solution was to separate us and put a Latinx person at the table of different committees. But no, I wasn't going to be the token Latina at the table just because it looks good to have a Latina at the table, especially if I'm not going to be listened to.

There was more we needed or could do outside of the scope of the Early Literacy committee. It was very rigid, everything had to be planned a certain way and had to go through this person, that then had to go through that other person. So, in one way, "Thank you, that was an awesome idea." But in another way, I felt it completely took away our whole entire voice as a committee.

Sheila: Speaking of that, I remember that members of the committee I was placed in pitched the idea of creating a community forum in which the public could come into the library and give ideas and feedback as to how the library could create better programming and services, particularly for underserved groups. This idea was immediately shut down because it meant that, "the people who attended would have too much say in what goes on in the library."

I often felt that top administration was working overtime to keep everything really rigid and only within the confines of the library while others actually took our feedback to heart. It was clear they also faced the exact same obstacles, like being told that they couldn't hold the community forum because they didn't want the community members to feel like they were running the library. We got the same response when, I think Angelo, had the similar idea to get the Latinx community to come in and speak to library administrators about their needs at the library.

Angelo: To be honest, that is why I invited the local Latino Coalition to have one of their monthly meetings[1] in the library because I knew that they were going to take that opportunity to really grill the library director and administrators, and confront them about our needs, and they did. Then I heard from different non-Latinx staff about how that was probably not the best thing to do, but in the back of my mind I thought, "Well, that's exactly why I did it."

I do agree with Sheila, that the top administrators were a very big obstacle. I think that there's some history to that. A lot of us were not aware of how they were and how they wanted to run the library. But again, I think you're totally correct, it comes down to this obsession with control and this fear of anybody else having any sort of say in how the library runs. Which brings up the question about how much of this has to do with structures. And the related question is, how are those structures related to racism? I don't have the answers, but I think those are the sort of big questions in the room.

Erica: That's basically it in a nutshell. I think racism is still well and alive in all of our institutions in that the library is typically a city government and local government institution. It isn't a surprise to any of us that those things are in place, especially in a library, because we are essentially the gatekeepers of information and of knowledge. We connect people to resources and information and it's that access to it that is controlled by all the rules and policies in place. They're designed for a certain group of people to be able to use the library more than others. My experiences showed me that in many ways. Then, when we do have groups that

---

1 The coalition did not have their own meeting space. Their organizing model was to ask local organizations to host them in exchange for the host having the chance to formally present about their services to meeting attendees. Angelo had been attending these meetings and arranged for them to hold one at the library.

want to reach out and branch out, we get those roadblocks. So I absolutely think it's systemic and I absolutely think that a lot of the barriers that we faced are not unique to our experience at all.

Sheila: Ok, so I know that we've talked about some of the negative experiences; are there any initial positives you would like to talk about?

Nephtali: Well, in the beginning I felt like we definitely had a positive start. Just meeting at Angelo's and eating and talking about what we could do for the community. That first year when we went to the church festivals and got our foot in the door, into the community, that felt great. It felt like we were going to start making a difference.

Sheila: I agree. I felt like the first year went really well. We did a lot but soon after, that momentum and support slowly died down. I don't know how that happened or why it happened, but maybe someone else has better insight into that.

Angelo: I mean, I think I made a lot of mistakes in my leadership that probably contributed. The mistakes that I made had to do with what I was saying previously about administration and the structures there. I was promoted to a position where I suddenly had a lot more on my plate that I frankly didn't really know how to handle. And, like many early career librarians I have since talked to, I suffered from both "imposter syndrome" and a lack of training. In a way, there was a little bit more freedom being a paraprofessional because I wasn't so involved or worried about structural things. But as soon as I became someone who was going to manage meetings, for example, I saw how they [administrators] were and I saw how they were making decisions and I saw what the barriers were and that contributed to a sort of anxiety in me that made me step back probably more than I should have. I think that played some kind of role for sure.

Erica: I also think it goes back to what I just said, in that they wanted a token Latinx person to fill in the spot. They wanted us at the table for representation but not for anything else beyond that. In a lot of the conversations that I'd have with my supervisor, I would have to explain, "Ok, I get it. Yes, we are a Latinx face, but it's more than that." To which her response was always some variation of, "Well, you guys are Latinx. You're there. You're represented." I understand that in her [the supervisor's] perspective, as I'm sure is the mentality of many top-level individuals, giving us a spot meant giving us a voice, but representation means nothing without power and change.

I completely agree that a lot of things were dumped on Angelo and we were looking to him for guidance because we were excited and wanted that leadership. We felt like him being in that position would give us a little bit more leverage. But he was also facing things that we didn't have any idea about. It would have been more beneficial for us to communicate more, for him even to vent with us and let us know these things because then we would have understood a little bit more what was going on behind the scenes and not felt so uncertain about things. I blame our out-of-sync schedules and lack of support in allowing us time to meet for that. In some situations he was able to be more vocal about things and in other situations he couldn't. As paraprofessionals, we didn't know either way because we had our "places" in which to stay.

Nephtali: I think that it also comes back to the misconception that Angelo by himself was supposed to be the advocate for all of the Latinx community and he couldn't possibly be that. None of us could.

Angelo: I think too, and what makes it complicated, is the feeling that as my first librarian experience, I was trying make an institution accountable to a specific community. That was a lot of pressure. Another thing I learned is that people in the community can also make some mistakes and it's important to mention this. Those mistakes relate to the fact that in the city, there are a number of divides within the Latinx community, especially between people with formal education and/or citizenship and people without formal education and/or who are not citizens. I was in a situation where I was hearing opposing things from people who think of themselves as leaders and that's bad enough in itself, but then how do you deal with those internal contradictions in an effective, safe, and productive way?

I remember when I was thinking long term about Día de Los Muertos[2]. Día de Los Muertos is so complicated. I mean, even in Mexico there are thousands of different opinions about what it is, how it's celebrated, when it's celebrated, and what you're supposed to do. When you take that already complicated situation and dump it on various immigrant groups in the community and try to get them to speak with one voice, it's going to be nearly impossible.

My long-term plan was to get people--Mexican folks--that were not in agreement about what Día de Los Muertos is, in the same room so that the conversation about these contradictions could happen between us. There would no doubt be some people in the community that were not going to be open to that because they were convinced that their understanding of Día de Los Muertos was the correct understanding. If you have one side of a community that's not necessarily united and on the other side, an institution that doesn't have enough representation for the diversity of those opinions to work them out, then you have a really bad situation. In many ways, that was the situation that we were in.

Sheila: So, overall, do you all feel we were successful in our efforts as the LAC?

Nephtali: To be honest, ever since Angelo, Sheila, and Erica left, I haven't heard anything whatsoever about continuing the Latinx Advisory Committee. It was discouraging to have the committee not be taken seriously anymore. However, I felt like the only thing that was successful is our inner determination to bridge the gap between the Latinx community and library resources. It may not happen with this library system right now, but it's something that I, myself, am determined to continue on with.

Angelo: This is my first time hearing the story about all of you being sent to different committees and there's a part of me, like a little rebel part of me that thinks that was a sign of success, right? That means that the top administrators were so afraid of what could have been done that they took that measure. In a certain way, there was potential for there to be success were it not for that intervention. I don't know,

---

2 For several years prior to the start of Sheila, Nephtali, Erica and Angelo's employment, the library had been organizing programming about Día de Muertos in late October/early November.

that's how I see it. The fact that we got together, went to the community festivals[3], initiated Spanish language story times, we did that for as long as we could...

Nephtali: Actually, it's still going on, sorry.

Angelo: Story times are still going on? I mean, that's a success in and of itself, right? So, the question on the table is: would that even had happened if we weren't so headstrong about it? Because, sure, the administration all wanted to do Spanish language story time, but they kept putting it off to "someday" because they let perfect be the enemy of good. They would say things like, "We can't because we have to make sure that we have the books. We have to make sure that if someone calls in sick, there's someone to cover. We have to make sure that..." All of these "ifs, ifs, ifs." In a sense, what we did was to be like, "You know, we just have to do it." And that's a success.

Nephtali: I agree with that. We know that we can do it because we did it and it was successful! All it takes is to step up and we did. So now, we move on to the next great thing from there.

Sheila: Erica, what do you think?

Erica: I think that we were successful in many ways that are going to be felt long-term. Our presence is key because we are advocates for our people. We were a very small group, but we pushed for necessary initiatives and got things done despite the barriers. It wasn't for anyone's personal gain, but as a whole we did really good things for the community that the library initially was not willing to give space for. In terms of the higher administration, I think we were successful in helping them realize they need to depend on those who they put next to them to assist them for more than just errands around the library or to be used in place of Google translate. We really had a voice and input and I think we added value and a perspective that

---

3 Each summer, Spanish-speaking churches have organized open-air, multi-day festivals. Members of the LAC felt a first priority for outreach to latinx communities was to be present as a library at these festivals.

they would not have access to were it not for our own unique experiences and backgrounds.

We were successful every time we went out into the community and every time we connected a family to library resources they didn't know were necessary or valuable for their lives. In a lot of ways, we broke many barriers by simply being a presence in an institution that doesn't typically give us a presence. When people from the community saw us speaking Spanish, for example, giving monthly interviews at a local Spanish radio station, they knew what we offered and what libraries we were at. They knew they could come to any of our branches and someone they could identify with would be there for them. That level of trust in an otherwise untrusting community is invaluable.

I don't believe there were failures because we didn't really have any expectations coming into the group other than, "What can we do to connect the community to the library?" Remember? That was our original motivator and we stayed true to that. We didn't have a guideline or say, "by this time this needs to be done, by that time this needs to be done." We just knew more needed to be done for us. The things we did accomplish are proof of the success we didn't even know we were going to have. That's my perspective in terms of our success.

Sheila: I agree with you all. I think that overall we were very successful. I do think we all wanted to do more. I feel like we had the potential to do more and I think that is probably what leads to some frustration and some of the feelings that there could have been so much more done. As a baseline we did a lot of great work that will probably keep going for some time to come. That said, I have one last question for you all and that is: If you could give advice to other groups--or maybe just an individual because a lot of times it's an individual who's doing this work--what kind of advice would you give to someone that's trying to advocate for change?

Erica: I would say surround yourself with individuals who are like-minded. Even if they're not in the library field with you, but people you know or those whom you see working with different groups. Don't be afraid to find other groups and see what worked for them and bring those ideas with you. Another thing is, it's going to feel lonely; we were all on an island on our own in a lot of situations. It's also going to feel like a lot of the work that you want to get done--you just have to do it first, and then present it. So be prepared for having to do a lot of work on your own, a lot of research and be prepared for the possibility of it getting shut down. Especially in a system that is kind of teetering on, "Yes, we want diversity", but not really committed to it. Be prepared to accept those "no's" and if you get rejected at first, don't give up! Go back to the drawing board if you have to and try again in another way. If this is something that you're passionate about, don't be afraid to go out there and present your ideas. Know what the possible benefits are, what the risks might be for that certain idea and be prepared to explain, "This is how we can work around it."

Angelo: Yeah, I like this practice of just being fearless. I need to hear that because I tend to be a very anxious person; I think that it's good advice. It reminds me of when I met with a veteran Latinx librarian from a nearby library system a few years ago and one of the things that she said to me was, "I just do things and if I get in trouble for it, if I get a lecture about it, whatever. At least I tried and at least I put something out there. I'd rather get in trouble for things that I tried than to play it safe." In practice this is very hard for me. It's important to point out that not everyone has the job security to know they'll get a lecture instead of, say, getting fired, but I think it's good advice for sure.

Nephtali: I can't really add anything more than what you all said besides that, it does help to be surrounded by people who have the passion and determination that you have going into whatever initiatives you want to start in your library system. I know that, for example, Erica's passion was a constant and a driving force in this group.

Sheila: I think one of the pieces of advice that I have is to really push for people to tell you about the things no one wants to talk about. I felt that strongly in the library, where nobody wanted to talk about things that happened in the past that influence politics now. It would have helped us if we knew some of these things in advance when trying to advocate to higher administration. We learned a bit about this in the last meeting I attended, where a library administrator told us, "We have tried this before and this before." It was surprising to find this out after all of the time and effort we put in the LAC. I had no idea that they'd tried similar things before because nobody ever mentioned it. Don't be afraid to be that person that asks a lot of questions. I often say that I can be annoying with my questions because I want or need to do something and my questions need to be answered for me to get it done.

Also, similar to what Erica--and all of you--were saying: be fearless. I think toward the end for me, I was really taking into account that this is a job. And I know for a lot of people this is a passion, it's a career. But it's not the only way you can fulfill your passion. It is one job, one way of many in which you can do what you're passionate about. That's my best advice.

Does anybody have anything else to add?

Angelo: I just want to add one more thing. I think one of the things that I learned while working with the local community is that it wasn't really taken seriously that everyone in the community has a right to the library and that it is, on paper, a democratic institution. It didn't seem like there was a lot of enthusiasm to run to be on the library Board. That was kind of frustrating for me because a lot of people were wanting to get involved in more private enterprises, but when you asked them to be on a board for an institution that provides free services for everybody, people weren't really enthusiastic. I think it's important to put out there that the community also has to do their part and one of the things that the community can do is really call the bluff on the fact that public libraries are "public" and run for the Board, and make it theirs[4].

Also, we forgot to mention how good the food was at meetings!

Nephtali: Oh yes, I miss that!

Erica: Yeah, another piece of advice: HAVE FOOD! Must have the following

---

4 While reviewing the transcript of this talk, Sheila made important points of clarification. She pointed out that communities that have not always had access to these kinds of resources can't be expected to value it to the extent we would like them to. She also called on us to recognize that library boards are essentially free labor for the common good and not everyone will agree to do this when they could be getting paid for their labor directly. Finally, two acquaintances did in fact agree to apply for a vacant board position but ultimately, were not chosen.

menu: rice, empanadas, tamales, chips, cake. You know, for brain purposes.

Nepthali: It was awesome.

Erica: Overall, I think these were all good points. The most important outcome from all of our efforts is we know that it works! We also know that if we had better resources, more support and time, greater things would've been accomplished. We confronted many obstacles, but still represented for the vital information and resource needs of our community. What we did as the LAC is something that can be repeated in any other library system and having committees like ours, with diverse and passionate leaders, is essential for the future of all libraries. That is my proudest realization when I think about the LAC.

While the work of the LAC did not continue in the way the founding members envisioned, it has strongly impacted their current paths in life. Nephtali continues to work in a public library, where she connects patrons to the resources they need and fulfills her passion of serving her community. Sheila now works in academic libraries, where her work focuses on community engagement. Erica has launched her own business, is now a substitute teacher in the inner city, and continues to work directly with her local community serving on various boards, implementing networking, community outreach and professional development events for young professionals of color, and serving on the leadership team of the City's Neighborhood Summit for the 3rd year in a row. Angelo also continues to work in libraries and has begun a career in international librarianship.

In contributing this chapter, the authors ultimately sought to empower other paraprofessionals to step out from behind the reference desk and become agents of change for the benefit of the communities they serve. It is the authors' sincere hope that their discussion provides good points of reference and that as individuals, they can serve as resources to the library community.

Art by Crystal Burgoyne, 2005
Hostage from Patriot Memory Game
Mixed Media
4"x5"x1/8"

Librarians With Spines Vol. II

Amira in America: A Graphic Pathfinder for Refugees

Andrea Castillo
Carmen A. Collins
Liz Laribee
Dolly Martino

Amira in America (https://thehornbakery.tumblr.com/) is a graphic pathfinder created to assist refugees experiencing resettlement. We aimed to create something that holds broader meaning with implications for the way academic librarians approach their work.

The story centers on Amira, a Syrian girl who is adjusting to life in her new American school, and her teacher, an immigrant from Ethiopia who came to the U.S. as a boy. By including the interaction between the two characters, we sought to capture a variety of experiences not limited to one gender, one country or one generation. We wanted to include a character from Syria (her country is not explicitly stated in the story, though we chose to use terms for grandmother and cat that would be used there) because of the influx of people into the U.S. from that country. Additionally, we wanted to represent the Ethiopian population that has resettled in the DC metro area in recent decades. The teacher was depicted as a man, as Kobel cites, 1992 refugee resettlement data indicated that 62 percent of the refugees in Ethiopia at the time were male. We also acknowledge that the interaction between a male teacher and a female student could be a departure from the lived experience of some, though we hope it could also provide an opportunity to discuss distinct cultural differences and some of the dynamics that arise when in a new host country. Inspiration for the story in the comic came from a variety of sources: from the story of a Syrian girl named Saja featured in a UNICEF video series called "Children of Syria Speak," to the 2007 novel "The Beautiful Things That Heaven Bears," the debut novel of Ethiopian immigrant Dinaw Mengestu whose protagonist migrates to Washington, D.C., from Ethiopia.

We made several creative choices throughout the design process aimed at better serving our target market of young refugees. For the format, we decided to create a comic, appreciating its ability to portray a narrative largely through the use of images, with the hopes of bridging language barriers. We looked to harness what Thomas et - al illuminated:

> "By pairing spare text with often powerful visual imagery, graphic novels offer a highly intimate look at real-world issues. Like movies, graphic novels are sensory and immersive; but like books, they require a degree of 'activeness' in the consumer's position. In their ideal form, [comics] combine the best of film and prose in delivering a cognitive and affective experience through which to access their subject matter" (2010).

We centered the narrative around a relatable character for young readers, and then we paired that narrative with a straightforward guide to information related to immigration and resettlement. Pairing the story with the pictures helps get the message across more easily, especially for those who may lack literacy skills, either in English or even in their own language. We hope that refugee children can relate to the story and in turn, show the comic to their parents or caregivers. Those adults can then contact the listed organizations or check the websites or other resources and connect with people or information that can be helpful to them. Our hope was to help guide our audience to a greater understanding of available resources; this prompted our choice to list the best and most consistent organizations equipped to provide comprehensive assistance to new refugees.

Additionally, we made the creative choice to color only certain pages within the comic and to leave the rest as coloring sheets. Research shows that refugee children who complete art-based programs and verbal-processing interventions have displayed lower rates of psychological distress (Tyrer & Fazel, 2014). By creating a comic that can be used as both a coloring book and a jumping-off point for constructive dialogue, we aim to facilitate a path in both directions. From personal field experience, one team member observed that children in a refugee environment benefited from structured creative activities that also allow for personal choice within that structure.

In order to expand its reach to our target audience, the next step for Amira in America is translation into different languages, focusing on the most prevalent within the DC metro area. Public documents in Washington, D.C. must be translated into six languages in addition to English: Amharic, Chinese, French, Korean, Spanish and Vietnamese (Ten Years of Language Access in Washington, DC). We also plan to translate the text into Arabic, the language of our central character.

Information, Culture, and User Needs: Background Research

Refugees and asylum-seekers face unique risks of instability and danger; in addition to the necessary and complex navigation of a new host country, they do so at a time and in a place marked with an increasing national conversation of racial divisions, Islamophobia, police brutality, and economic instability. The State Department reports that women and children comprise more than 72 percent of the current refugee population in the U.S. The report goes on to describe particular complexities and needs of the group, highlighting that "many are single mothers, survivors of torture, people who need urgent medical treatment, religious minorities, lesbian, gay, bisexual, transgender, or intersex (LGBTI) persons, or others imperiled by violence and persecution." The American Library Association's description of its outreach resources for people of color emphasizes that the availability of and access to the kinds of resources, services and technologies typically found in a library become critically important in a refugee's life; it touches on the difficulties of language barriers, cultural isolation, racism or discrimination based on appearance, documentation, status, etc., to illustrate the particularly high stakes for refugees in a new country.

In FY2015, there were more than 5,000 people classified as refugees living in Washington, D.C., Virginia and Maryland, according to the U.S. Department of Health and Human Services' Office of Refugee Resettlement. According to the Office of Refugee Resettlement, Washington, D.C. is one of the American cities that hosts the smallest number of resettled refugees due to its high cost of living. This factor pitches those refugees that do settle in the area into a particularly fragile economic stability.

The Office of the United Nations High Commissioner for Refugees (UNHCR) estimated that one in every 113 people on earth sought asylum in 2015. The catalyst for emigration, oftentimes cataclysmic events like war, famine and poverty, and the statistically likely reality of political and social upheaval in their countries, result in a high percentage of depression and PTSD in refugees. Studies showing a 10 to 40 percent and a 5 to 15 percent incidence, respectively, according to the Massachusetts-based Refugee Health Technical Assistance Center, are even higher for children refugees, with an incidence of 50 to 90 percent for PTSD and 6 to 40 percent rate of depression.

The resettlement process within a new country's particularities requires orienting into a new "information landscape" or "intersubjective space" as described by Lloyd, Kennan, Thompson, and Qayyum. A critical piece of navigation is that of compliance to distinct, and perhaps seemingly arbitrary, rules and policies of a new country, new standards for licensing, and strict tenets for applying for and maintaining visas (Lloyd et al, 2013). It also requires orientation as to how to seek meaningful life information such as employment, how to find a primary care provider, how and where to enroll their children into school, etc. This process is of course complicated dramatically for refugees who struggle with literacy or do not already speak the dominant language.

One study explores the factor of digital literacy among refugee and immigrant groups, highlighting that many are unable to afford computers or other platforms that would grant them Internet access; additionally, many more still maintain distrust for government institutions and systems as well as the Internet (Lloyd et al., 2013).

Lloyd et al link information literacy to the likelihood of a successful transition:

"A lack of access to information creates conditions and barriers that prohibit full participation in education, work, and everyday life. Consequently, those without access to information run the risk of becoming increasingly excluded from mainstream information sources and may fail to develop the capacity to fully settle, to recognize and take up opportunities, and to participate in society as full citizens" (p. 123-4).

Another probable barrier to information seeking is the mental health of the individual refugee during resettlement. Mental health issues among refugees are often relegated to afterthoughts, even though their presence could and likely does affect every step of integration into a new culture (Fazel, Reed, Panter-Brick, and Stein, 2012). Another is that many refugees lack the financial resources, navigable knowledge, transportation, and time to make mental health a priority during their transition.

Cultural Representation in Comics: Applicability of Comic Media in Libraries

Diverse children's literature is critically important because it allows children of all backgrounds to see themselves and their experiences reflected in books. When children can see themselves mirrored in the books, three things happen. First, reading becomes a far more engaging proposition for those students. Second, children consider libraries with a diverse book collection to be welcoming and safe spaces where they can find validation, have positive experiences, and feel respected. And third, these books can serve as an inspiration for all children to pursue their dreams and see that others have blazed the trail before them. Reading about the lives and accomplishments of others like them will help to instill confidence that they are valued and honored in the library, the school, and the community.

Diverse books provide more than just a mirror for children from underrepresented groups to see themselves. They also provide windows into the perspectives of these groups, allowing people who are not from that group to understand more and to realize that all people have more in common than we thought. As Tschida, Ryan, & Ticknor (2014) explain, "Books are sometimes the only place where readers may meet people who are not like themselves, who offer alternative worldviews." They go on to expound on this theory, popularized by Bishop (1990), that diverse books serve as both mirrors and windows, emphasizing that we all need both: books that are mirrors reflecting our own lives and books that are windows into the lives of others. Bishop (2012) later goes on to state: "children have a right to books that reflect their own images and books that open less familiar worlds to them." Diverse books help us break free of the persistent white, middle class perspective that is the singular predominant story in our textbooks, history books, and indeed throughout literature (and media), providing a more complex and often conflicting view of the events.

Although most librarians welcome diverse books for children, incorporating diverse comic literature in library collections hasn't been as widespread until recently. Comics featuring diverse main characters are beginning to obtain more visibility, with recent titles such as Pashmina by Nidhi Chanani, The Shadow Hero by Gene Luen Yang, and the March series by Congressman John Lewis and Andrew Aydin. And the comic/graphic novel genre itself is only starting to achieve more acceptance and respect within the community.

Industrywide, the American Library Association promotes graphic novels in libraries through the Will Eisner Graphic Novel Grants for Libraries, which support libraries seeking to expand existing graphic novel support services and programs, as well as libraries initiating a graphic novel service, program or initiative. Recent examples of award-winning projects include one at the University of Colorado Springs aimed at more inclusivity for veterans, to include a series of creative workshops and an expanded graphic novel collection, as well as another at Tuscarawas County Public Library System in Ohio aimed at motivating girls in grades 3-12 to enhance their media literacy skills, further develop their emotional intelligence, and discover new ways to engage with literature while reading female-driven graphic novels (American Library Association, 2018).

However, this mainstream acceptance of comics and graphic novels among librarians, teachers and others was a long time coming. Many working as information professionals in the 1940s and 1950s at the height of popularity for comic books—including librarians, teachers and community leaders—did not always see their potential, worrying more about their influence on children's moral development and steering them toward what was viewed as more educational and respectable reading. It would take decades after the Comics Magazine Association of America created the Comics Code Authority in 1954, serving as a censor for mainstream comic titles, for the medium to develop respectability in many circles. Even when librarians began to embrace comics and graphic novels as a way to bring in reluctant readers and those with reading difficulties such as dyslexia, many regarded comics as "entertaining junk" (Nyberg, 2010). However, in response to the censors, underground comics with more political and socially conscious themes flourished in the 1970s and 1980s, seeing the publication of titles like Will Eisner's A Contract with God and Other Tenement Stories, Frank Miller's Batman: The Dark Knight Returns, Alan Moore and Dave Gibbons' Watchmen, and Art Spiegelman's Maus: A Survivor's Tale (Carleton, 2014).

Not only can librarians provide patrons with comics and graphic novels, which can address varying literacy and communications needs, as well as comics that talk about social issues, they can also more readily embrace their role as educators, offering library programming such as ESL courses or information sessions about navigating life in their new country, as well as connecting them with community partners who can aid in that effort. A librarian's knowledge of her collection, combined with a more proactive teaching or educational approach, can help keep the profession relevant to users in an evolving informational environment (Bell & Shank, 2004).

While graphic novels and comics can be used to build literacy in the traditional text-based sense, it can also be used to develop literary analysis skills, as well as teach users how to interpret meaning when text and visuals are combined, developing multimodal literacy. With both text and illustrations in comics, readers get a depth of meaning that is not possible with just words or images alone (Jacobs, 2013). While the words are certainly helpful to build traditional text-based literacy, the images of a gesture or facial expression of a character in the comic can convey meaning beyond the limits of the words. Others in the field have used multimodal tools in educational environments, teaching teens to use iPad animations to convey and interpret emotion (Mills & Unsworth, 2017) and building student engagement among sixth graders studying health through lessons involving text, Internet and other media (Casey, 2012). The concept of literacy beyond text is especially important with our audience, as they may be struggling with literacy in English, or even in their native languages. This medium also has the advantage of presenting more diverse voices to users than more traditional texts often do (Schwarz, 2006).

Visual resources such as comics and graphic novels can be especially helpful for refugees, asylum-seekers and immigrants who are learning to get around in a new country. Researchers in Australia found that when developing functional literacy in the new environment, some refugees found value in relying on items like shopping catalogs and store flyers to plan grocery purchases, DVDs and magazines to connect to new information, play money to learn Australian currency and make a budget, and even watching other people helped pick up cues about everyday activities (Lloyd et al., 2013, p. 133-4).

In considering audiences outside of our target market, we see Amira in America as having the potential to be a catalyst for broader understanding and empathy, especially for young audiences. We have a distinct interest in the ways in which comics can harness the attention of young readers, especially in the context of the library as a learning site. Part of that comes with paving a new path toward representation. The visual scope within Amira in America is a dramatic departure from the visuals typically available to the average American child, and it is by using that representation that we hope to prompt empathic investment, particularly at a critical age. The character of Amira is just slightly younger than the age group at which students develop a disinterest in traditional education. "During the middle school years, youth tend to become less motivated to learn" (Harter, Whitesell, & Kowalski, 1992). The opportunity that this project focuses on is the use of comics as an educational tool, exploring the ways in which this format fosters active engagement from students, sparks creative processes in conjunction with rote learning, and possesses the ability to accommodate a wide range of reading level, education level, and cultural background. Interest, or the motivation to learn, is a principal factor in the learning process. Education research suggests that motivation for learning is influenced more by the context of learning than by the age-specific attitudes of the participants (Anderman & Maehr, 1994; Wigfield, Eccles, & Rodriguez, 1998). This echoes the findings of Dawes and Larson (2011) that even if interest is not a primary motivator for participation, interest can be developed. Ultimately, the use of comics as an empathy builder has the potential to be a game changer in the field of library science.

Librarians can also leverage their research skills and knowledge, as well as community ties and knowledge of community needs to develop appropriate resources; in this case, for refugees and asylum-seekers, as well as other users for whom librarians see the need. In this way, as Doherty describes, "a new picture of libraries may begin to emerge: content creators, rather than content hoarders" (2007). If librarians embrace these roles, not only as custodians of materials, but also as educators and even creators of resources, it could transform the way the public views the role of libraries in their communities.

Conclusion

Given the current political climate in the U.S., refugees may feel as insecure as ever about their status here. For children, who are the powerless and often voiceless participants in the conflict that drove them from home, this insecurity can be displayed through signs of withdrawal, depression, or even poor behavior. Through Amira in America, we hope to reach refugee children with a simple story they can find comfort in, provide them an opportunity in which to be creative by coloring and drawing, and list resources available locally and globally. Our ultimate goal is to reach out to these children through their parents, teachers, religious leaders, and caregivers and start the discussion to deliver those services in the path toward providing much-needed support and security. Newly arrived refugees in our country are among the most vulnerable people within our borders. Their search for information is closely linked to their very survival. This population calls for the best of what we can offer in terms of resources and hospitality. Libraries have been the site of critical services and opportunities for newly arrived refugees, and the opportunity to expand and improve these services is upon us. It will be incredibly important to establish culturally competent systems to absorb the influx of refugees into this country. Refugee services ought to take a higher priority for information professionals; proactive progress is the way to move ahead and serve the mission of this profession.

"Amira in America by the Hornbakery"

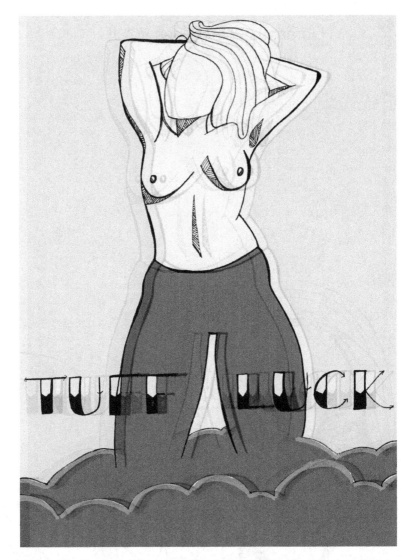

"'Tuff Luck' was created shortly after one of the most challenging years of my life. A domino effect of stressful circumstances, broken hearts and 5 moves worth of change. On top of that, I was diagnosed with MS-the day before I was set to move to a new city where I didn't really know anyone.

While I was coping with a new medical diagnosis, city, apartment and life... I was also healing from a verbally and emotionally abusive relationship. Body shaming in that relationship was fairly rampant. As a body positive artist, I became very aware of how the body shaming had started to chip away at my self worth and I pushed back with art. When I drew Tuff Luck, I decided to embrace who I was at that very moment: hurt, alone, scared, changed- but also tough. I made the choice to leave someone toxic, start new somewhere alone and carry a heavy diagnosis with me. And despite the stress of it all, I felt pretty damn awesome and more connected to myself than I had been in a long time."

-Amy Willis
www.libidobidil.com

Takeaways from the Hampton LIS Forum

Miguel Juárez, PhD
Jina DuVernay
Rebecca Hankins, CA

January 11, 2019

The Hampton University LIS Forum on Minority Recruitment and Retention in the Library & Information Science field (henceforth called the Forum) was presented August 1-2, 2018 at the William R. and Norma B. Harvey Library, Hampton University in Hampton, VA. The Forum addressed issues on the recruitment, retention and promotion of librarians of color which are pertinent today. In 1927, the First Conference of Negro Librarians was held at Hampton College in Hampton, VA. There were substantial issues regarding the recruitment of diverse librarians in 1927, as there are now, 91 years later. According to the essay Librarians in the United States from 1880-2009, the first census record of "a non-white librarian was in 1920; in 1950, there were 990 African American librarians, representing two percent of the total librarian population."[1] As noted on the application by Hampton College to the Institute for Museums and Library Services (IMLS), "the most recent demographic data from ALA (2014) shows that the profession remains largely white with only 12.9% of survey respondents self-identifying as minorities. This shows only a 2.9% increase in diversity over a 16-year period." It is evident that we have more work to do concerning diversifying the library profession.

The Forum was organized by Hampton University Library Director Tina D. Rollins, funded by the Institute of Museum and Library Services (IMLS), a government agency that, among its funding goals, is the strategic work of recruitment and retention of librarians. The Forum was divided into the following three groups of participants: Group 1 was comprised of the committee under Rollins who sought funding, organized the conference, and participated at the conference by introducing speakers, etc. Some of those individuals included Dr. Pauletta Brown Bracy, LaTisha Lankford, Judy Allen Dodson, and Jamar Rahming. Group 2 were presenters who were contacted a year before the event took place, were solicited for letters of support, and agreed to participate in various panels. Group 3 consisted of 50 selected library professionals who competed to attend based on an essay submission which indicated their interest in diversity in the

---

1 Beveridge, Andrew A. et. al. Librarians in the United States from 1880-2009. Oxford University Press's Academic Insights for the Thinking World. June 20th, 2011. Reviewed 1-10-19, https://blog.oup.com/2011/06/librarian-census/

LIS field. All of the selected participants were provided with lodging and some meals. Attendees were required to participate in a webinar before the conference and were provided with a reading list which included titles authored by members of the panel. In addition, Harvey Library staff members were involved in running the highly successful and transformative event.

The Forum was an opportunity for the diverse attendees to discuss diversity issues in a safe, welcoming space at a HBCU (a college or university that was originally founded to educate students of African-American descent) with a long history of support for librarians of color. According to Rollins, the purpose of the Forum was to "identify critical issues in the recruitment, retention and promotion of minority librarians." A white paper will be produced on the proceedings which will offer "new strategies to improve minority representation in libraries and Information Science." The Forum consisted of presentations by speakers over the course of two days, a panel discussion and a second-day speaker presentation followed by an afternoon strategy session.

Director Rollins opened the Forum by introducing Campus President Dr. William R. Harvey who welcomed us to the meeting. After Dr. Harvey spoke, Dr. Pauletta Brown went over the ground rules for the two-day event. Her comments were followed by a presentation by Dr. Ismail Abdullahi, North Carolina Central University LIS Professor. A "Lunch and Learn" session was presented by Ms. Rebecca Hankins, Archivist/Librarian, Texas A&M University; Dr. Miguel Juárez, University of Texas at El Paso; and Dr. Nicole Cooke, Associate Professor in the School of Information Science, University of Illinois at Urbana-Champaign. An afternoon session was conducted by Dr. Angela Spranger, Lecturer in Management, Christopher Newport University. The closing session for the first day was presented by Wanda Kay Brown, ALA's 2019-2020 President Elect. A reception and tour of the Hampton University Museum, which is the oldest African American museum in the United States founded in 1868, followed the closing session, http://museum.hamptonu.edu/.

On the morning of the second day, Mark Puente, Director of Diversity and Leadership Programs, Association of Research Libraries (ARL) presented on "The State of Recruitment of Minority Librarians." Following Puente's presentation, participants engaged in a strategy session to determine our next moves and to see what issues we should focus our efforts on for future discussions and/or forums. Participants in the Forum included librarians, library directors and LIS educators from Alabama, Florida, Georgia, Illinois, Minnesota, New York, North Carolina, Oregon, South Carolina, Texas, Virginia, and Washington, D.C.

A follow-up conference call was held by Director Rollins after the Forum, where participants were encouraged to publish articles about the event to promote and publicize the outcomes of the conference. For this article, the co-authors answered the following questions:

- What expectations did you have about the Forum? Were your expectations realized? Why or why not?

- What in your opinion was significant about the Forum?

- Was it important for the Forum to take place at an HBCU? Why or why not?

- Could the Forum be held anywhere?

- Did you think it was important to keep the attendance level low?

- What did you think of the kinds of attendees to the Hampton LIS Forum?

- Which sessions did you find more meaningful?

- Which sessions did you find least useful or insightful?

- What do you think was lacking at the Forum?

- What would you had done differently?

- As a newer librarian, do you feel it addressed needs you might have as a professional?

- As a seasoned librarian, do you feel it addressed needs you might have as a professional?

- What do you think were the takeaways from the Forum?

- How do you think the Forum will be seen by individuals who did not attend? What do you need to know about the Forum which may not be apparent in the upcoming video or white paper?

Miguel Juárez, PhD, Adjunct Professor
University of Texas at El Paso and
El Paso Community College

What expectations did you have about the Hampton LIS Forum?
Were your expectations realized? Why or why not?

I had expectations that participants would share their diverse experiences

Dr. Pauletta Brown Bracy, Professor at North Carolina Central University and Dr. Miguel Juárez, at the Hampton Forum. Photograph courtesy of Miguel Juárez.

concerning diversity in the LIS profession. What I did not expect was the bonding which occurred between attendees. No one could have prepared us for the transformative experience we would have being part of the Forum. I likened the experience of it being a safe space with individuals who were almost like family and with people who were there to learn how we could create true change to diversify the LIS field. Participants were able to let their guard down, share themselves and their personal views on diversifying the field. I think the event was a great success and I look forward to future ones, as well as the reaction of librarians who were not able to attend the event or did not know about it. There are plans to upload the full video of the Forum in the near future, https://hamptonu.libguides.com/hulisforum.

What in your opinion was significant about the Forum?

The forum provided a safe space to share our painful stories of working in Predominantly White Institutions (PWIs). There were participants who stated that they had to leave their families behind to work in a library where they were the only librarian of color working in a PWI. The rich experience of attending the Forum also provided the opportunity to hear from numerous individuals who have long labored to increase diversity in libraries which included the attendees, as well as scholars like Dr. Pauletta Brown Bracy, Director of the Office of University Accreditation at North Carolina Central University, a few library directors of color and newer librarians as well as archivists and special collections librarians.

Library Conference, Hampton Institute, 1927. Photograph courtesy of William R. and Norma B. Harvey Library.

Was it important for the Forum to take place at an HBCU? Why or why not?

My attendance at the Forum provided a great opportunity to engage with librarians of color who shared similar experiences regarding diversity or the lack of diversity in libraries. Some of the librarians were the only persons of color in their libraries. Others had experienced a myriad of issues given the profession is predominantly white. Because the Forum was geographically based, a majority of the attendees were African American. The conference also attracted participants from Florida, Texas, Oregon and Washington, D.C. It was important that the Forum take place at an HBCU because it recreated the aforementioned 1927 meeting. At the same time, the organizers wanted to expand on the inaugural meeting by inviting participants from other backgrounds. In comparison to other library conferences, whites were the minority at the meeting.

Could the Forum be held anywhere?

There are other conferences and forums which address diversity in the profession such as the Joint Conference on Librarians of Color, the ALA Forum on Diversity, etc. Having the Forum at an HBCU is one of those lenses. These are conversations which are ongoing--and in my opinion, need to happen everywhere. Ideas and outcomes generated at the Forum can be presented as formal programs at our larger professional organizations such as ALA, ARL, ACRL, SAA and PLA. The Forum could have been held anywhere, but that it happened at Hampton University, was special.

Did you think it was important to keep the attendance level low?

I think it was a good strategy to keep the attendance low because it allowed individuals to interact with each other. When the forum began, participants sat where they wanted and where they felt most comfortable.

What did you think of the kinds of attendees to the Hampton LIS Forum?

There was a wealth of talent and experience in the room, but it would have been good to have more time to learn from others. I was grateful that I met Dr. Pauletta Brown Bracy, Associate Professor in the School of Library and Information Science at North Carolina Central University in Durham, North Carolina. She is a specialist in Young Adult Literature. I probably would have never met her if I had not been invited to present at the Forum. A number of attendees at the event had been her library school students and she was their mentor. I could see how Dr. Bracy and I might collaborate on researching how Young Adult Literature differs among African Americans and Latinx children, as well as other issues in the profession. In conjunction, we invited Jina DuVernay, Special Collections Librarian at Alabama State University's Levi Watkins Learning Center to write this article with us. Ms. DuVernay had come up to the podium and asked how she could begin to write about the profession after our panel on the first day. I decided that this was an opportunity to put our words into action, so I invited her to write the essay with us. We believe it is also important to bring others with us in our journey and to forge intergenerational connections with others making their way in the profession.

Which sessions did you find more meaningful?

I found the opening session extremely powerful. We went around the room and introduced ourselves. Attendees came from all parts of the country and as far away as Oregon and Texas. It also gathered a cadre of newer voices who had not been assembled in one place aside from JCLA, ALA, etc. It also attracted others who have graduated with their doctorate in LIS education as well as in other fields. It included newer librarians as well as experienced professionals. In many ways the Forum was an anomaly, an event which does not happen every year. But should.

Which sessions did you find least useful or insightful?

Personally, I was a bit disappointed to learn that with the resources ARL has at its disposal--including the consideration that they had recently held their diversity conference--they did not have a solid strategy to radically improve the numbers of librarians of color in the profession. This leads me to believe that recruiting, retaining and promoting librarians of color is a long-term, multi-decade issue with implications for librarians at all levels to include recruitment at entry and mid-levels, as well as administrative ones. We need to strive to impact the profession by advocating for its transformation to reflect current demographics.

As promoters of diversity in the profession, we can conduct outreach in the cities where we meet during library conferences. We can partner with school districts and visit area public schools, community colleges and universities to talk about the LIS profession. Universities are important; it is not common knowledge that to be a librarian requires a Master of Arts degree from accredited institutions. To only focus on increasing diversity at entry levels or at the LIS professorate levels where very little change occurs is short-sighted; it does not lead to broad-base and sustained change. In order to change the present course of diversity in libraries we need to start at the top with library leadership. We also need to step up against white privilege and colonization which occurs in PWIs and use different models which foster and support sustained diversity at all levels.

What do you think was lacking at the Forum?

With the wealth of experience in the room, it would have been great to have more time to interact with attendees at other tables. A pre- or post-conference dinner with attendees would have been good, but I understand the conference was at best, a three-day event, factoring travel time to and from the meeting. For those of us who traveled further from the region, two travel days and two days were required to attend the conference. I was really impressed with the work of the Hampton University staff and their ideas to make the conference a better experience. Library staff went out of their way to make us feel comfortable during the Forum. I believe that what set the Forum apart was the intimacy of our experiences. Library staff members acted like family, looking out for us and making sure our needs were met. The day many of us left, library staff checked-in our luggage at the library as if we were checking in baggage at the hotel, which made it much easier for many of us who had to rush to the airport after the last session. I found that small gesture of checking baggage into the library to be not only very innovative but also very thoughtful. It is important to create these kinds of positive and proactive settings for conferences which discuss race.

What would you had done differently?

I think the Forum worked well in its setting, but I believe it needs to be expanded and presented at national conferences with attendees who attended the first meeting along with others who may be interested in the expansion on the dialogue of developing strategies to address diversity in the profession. Different ideas are needed to develop sustained, long-term efforts.

As a newer librarian, do you feel it addressed needs you might have as a professional?

I think the meeting benefitted both newer and seasoned librarians. The Forum brought together a large group of librarians, library directors, HR professionals, library science faculty members, library program recruiters, etc. to engage in a "think tank" format and develop strategies to recruit, retain and promote librarians of color for libraries.

As a seasoned librarian, do you feel it addressed needs you might have as a professional?

As an experienced librarian with a doctoral degree, more than ever, it is imperative that I remain involved in diversity efforts and programs via research and publication, as well as presentations at conferences including mentoring and co-writing with newer librarians in the profession. Jina DuVernay, who contributed to this article, approached me after our panel at the Forum and asked me how she could get involved with writing about the conference and what she could write about. I invited her to write with Rebecca Hankins and myself for Max Macias' and Yago Cura's co-edited book, Librarians with Spines, Volume 2 which seeks to foster innovative and cutting-edge dialogues in the library profession.[2] In writing about this important conference, we also need to include newer voices in the profession in the hope they will continue where we left off.

---

2 This article "Takeaways from the Hampton LIS Forum, August 1-2, 2018 at Hampton University," is the first published article on the Hampton LIS Forum.

What do you think were the takeaways from the Forum?

The Forum was a disruption of what has happened in diversity conferences in the past. It was disruptive because it did not put on a dog and pony show. Attendance was limited to a smaller participation; it sought to have attendees make one-to-one connections, promoted a family-like approach and allowed more face time with mentors. Disruptions in the way things have been done concerning diversity issues will help create change and innovation for the future.

How do you think the Forum will be seen by individuals who did not attend?

The Forum was streamed, but individuals who did not attend it will be able to watch it on video when it is posted. However, they will miss the powerful presence which was in the room at the opening morning session the first day, along with the vibrant and insightful conversations which occurred at each table. Imagine being in a room with over 50 individuals who made time to attend a conference to listen to stories about the issues with diversifying the LIS profession and then who stayed a second day to brainstorm on strategies to increase diversity. Everyone at each table was involved in having honest and open discussions. In addition, the Forum was an event of many minds in a place of historic significance.

What do you need to know about the Forum which may not be apparent in the upcoming video or white paper?

People need to know that we need to have many more meetings like the Forum. It must not be a one-time event; solving the diversity crisis is not a one-year fix. With rising demographics, we need to develop strategies to increase the numbers of people of color in librarianship at all levels. I believe the Forum concept promises to change the mode of operation for sustained recruitment, retention and promotion of librarians of color. It is the model we can consider following because, unfortunately, everything else before it has not worked.

Rebecca Hankins, Associate Professor and Certified Archivist Librarian

Cushing Memorial Library and Archives

Texas A&M University Libraries

What expectations did you have about the Forum?

My expectations for the Forum were enumerated in my letter of support to IMLS on behalf of this event. The letter spoke about the necessity to continue to fund these types of timely forums, especially in these times when we see the greying of the profession, there is a need to find multiple and intentional ways to address this current "brain drain." The Forum would and should offer alternative approaches to recruitment and retention of librarians. Some examples I provided included finding opportunities to promote the library as a welcoming and inclusive institution by sponsoring diverse discussions such as panels (international librarians' and disabled librarians' experiences), webinars (ARL-AULS multi-part series on Stories of Inclusion: Inclusive Practices at Cultural Institutions), and workshops such as one presented at my institution on Implicit Bias led by Dr. Kate Ratliff. I also reiterated that IMLS has supported the strategic work of libraries and librarians and the Forum fits within the mission and values of their programming.

Were your expectations realized? Why or why not?

I do feel the majority of my expectations were met in many ways that included the opportunity to participate, share, and collaborate with a wide group of colleagues. The pace of sharing information on the format of panels and presentations to us, the presenters, could have been better and would have allowed for more time to prepare an engagement exercise (Appendix C) that we eventually had to scrap due to lack of time. We were not told in advance that there would be three of us on a panel and that a large chunk of that 2-hour time slot was going to include eating lunch. We learned that our panel would be a conversation about our personal roles as practitioners and experts in the field. Ms. Rollins provided us with the questions we were to respond to that resulted in a discussion that was more emotional and spoke to our everyday experiences as people of color working in predominantly white environments, rather than hypotheticals. It was much more a conversation about how we navigate these institutions that often marginalize our work and silence our voices. I had a number of people contact me and say how much it meant to them to hear our stories. The overall survey showed that our luncheon discussion was the second-best session of the 2-day Forum!

What in your opinion was significant about the Forum?

There were so many significant parts of the Forum. I'm always impressed when I meet experienced and new colleagues in the field. I'm a people person, so it is always important to make connections, see how we can support someone in the field, and provide a voice to those voices that have been silenced. I know that's always my message. Diversity is important and in spite of some discussion on how we should minimize representation, this Forum proved that it matters. People need to see themselves represented in the profession, especially when we are talking about recruitment and retention. No one that I know wants to be the token person of color in any environment including the LIS field.

Was it important for the Forum to take place at an HBCU? Why or why not?

Dr. Ismail Abdullahi spoke eloquently and provided a history lesson on Black librarianship that focused on Hampton University's unique and early history of librarian education for African Americans. Hampton University was the appropriate venue to serve as the foundation for the Forum. And this qoute was always in our thoughts about this small HBCU's history taken from their website:

> *"Hampton University holds a unique place in library science history through its historical library school. The Hampton Library School was founded in September 1925 by a grant from the Carnegie Corporation. The first and only library school for Negroes to issue a bachelor's degree in library science was accredited by the Board of Education for Librarianship of the American Library Association and therefore, became a member of the Association of American Library Schools. The library school program lasted until 1939 when it was sadly cut due to lack of funding."*

The importance of Hampton and HBCUs as a place for the Forum was reinforced after hearing from the incoming 2019-2020 ALA President Wanda Brown talk about how she made the decision to move from a private well-funded institution to an HBCU with little funding--inspiring talk from a veteran in the field. The wonderful support from the Hampton University staff, students, and administrators to the Mayor of Hampton--you knew this was important to the entire community.

Lastly, I loved the idea of recreating the class picture of the first librarians conference held at Hampton in March 15-18, 1927, that made us all aware of the solemn legacy of this institution and the importance that we, who stand in its shadows, ensure that this legacy continues.

Hampton University LIS Forum on Minority Recruitment and Retention in the Library & Information Science Field attendees in front of the William R. and Norma B. Harvey Library, Hampton University, in Hampton, VA. Photograph courtesy of William R. and Norma B. Harvey Library. 2018

Could the Forum be held anywhere?

As stated above, the legacy must continue. It is not a matter of can the Forum be held anywhere, but why should it? The iconic photos of the commemoration of La Raza Unida Convention participants in El Paso or the Harlem living legends of jazz photo can be taken in other places, but do they have the same impact, beauty and evocative feelings if taken somewhere else? It is the place and the participants that recognize the invaluable historical legacy of recreating these iconic events. I have participated in numerous discussions on diversity and inclusion in the profession and there needs to be more. Democracy continues to be a work in progress and so is diversity in our country!

Did you think it was important to keep the attendance level low?

Keeping the attendance low allows for more in-depth discussion and exercises that don't become unwieldy and unsatisfactory. I think having too many people dilutes the impact and there will be many that come away feeling that they did not get a chance to fully participate. At the beginning of the event everyone introduced themselves, a feat that would have taken much longer if there were

Attendees at the Forum pictured above (from left to right) included Sandra Riggs, Research and Instruction Librarian at the University of Georgia Libraries; Rory Patterson, Associate Dean, Planning, Administration, and Operations, Jerry Falwell Library; and Sony Prosper, the Diversity Alliance Resident at the University of Virginia. Photograph courtesy of Rebecca L. Hankins. 2018.

more than the small group in attendance. If we want to expand attendance, first you need sufficient funding and then you need to settle on one discussion point if you really want to make any progress. Keeping the attendance level low allowed for us to tackle two issues--recruitment and retention that often go hand in hand.

What did you think of the kinds of attendees to the Forum?

They were wonderful and diverse, both national and international, from different areas of librarianship; directors, instructors, professors, and practitioners attended the forum. I also liked that there were human resource experts, data specialists, historians, archivists, and many others who could speak to other opportunities within the LIS field, areas some of the attendees may not have considered as career options.

Which sessions did you find more meaningful?

I enjoyed all of the sessions, but the most meaningful were the history lessons that Dr. Abdullahi discussed and Tina's introduction that spoke about what she wanted this Forum to provide--concrete ways to impact recruitment and retention.

Dr. Angela Spranger's exercise in identity formation and how we see ourselves was very meaningful and very insightful. It said so much about who we are and the often difficult decisions we make when we talk about ourselves. After throwing away my African American, female, professor, intelligent labels I was left with one--Muslim. It's important because all of the other characteristics are visible; although I wear a khimar (Muslim headscarf) I am rarely identified as Muslim. One other colleague talked similarly about her heritage of being a Black Latino; we bonded over the invisibility within our own religious and ethnic groups. Who are we really after we strip away the labels? That was an eye-opener and very profound for me!

Which sessions did you find least useful or insightful?

I can't say any were least useful or insightful; they were all very good and touched on some aspect of the LIS process. It would have been productive to have more of a discussion about data in the LIS field. Mark Puente gave data regarding LIS education and graduates. His perspective was that the data shows a steady rate of diverse populations who are going into the LIS profession, but that the graduation rates will never reach any sort of parity with whites or that the percentages of people of color in the profession will move significantly. We were left to ponder whether we should conform to the lack of diversity or continue to strive to change the field. There wasn't much of a discussion afterwards about his presentation or how we can use that data to fight for diversifying the profession and more importantly, what data are we missing. The data didn't address recruitment strategies that work or don't work, the barriers and impacts such as funding, closing of LIS programs within communities of color, and environmental issues that many face when deciding on careers.

What do you think was lacking at the Forum?

Someone mentioned that there were no decision makers attending-- deans, directors, or department heads, but that negates and reduces the people who were there to cogs or just workers. We all have the ability and opportunity to be leaders, no matter what our positions. For this Forum, the attendance of experts in human resources, practitioners, scholars--and yes, there were directors and Deans--was an important first step in the process. Many of us are in the trenches and know the pitfalls; we've had to subvert, side-step, and jump over them. Our experiences offered the insights needed to start the dialogue and not reinvent the wheel. I think we could say, "Here's what we have experienced in the recruitment and retention process, here's what you are missing, and this is what is needed to do better." Similar to many other disciplines, particularly the STEM fields, the library needs to start investing in grow-your-own programs that start at the elementary level. We need to engage young people, providing them with examples of the variety of work we can do with LIS expertise. From subject experts in any field, data management, medical assistance where one goes on rounds with doctors providing data and information crucial to patient health, public librarianship, university professors, scholars, library directors/deans, and international travel throughout the world, librarianship builds your skills and experiences that allows each person to become a positive change-agent.

As an example, I spoke about my travels as an archivist and librarian all over the world to places as diverse as Amman, Jordan and Seoul, South Korea, to Bogor Cibinong, Indonesia and London, England where I have spoken on my research and the LIS profession. I have given presentations to elementary and high school students about being appointed to the National Historical Publications and Research Commission (NHPRC) by President Barack Obama, something that many of these students see as unimaginable.[3] These are a few of the exciting discussions we can have with students, at any level, to entice them into the LIS field.

What would you have done differently?

In a recent interview for a senior administrative position it was asked of me, what would I do to support my staff, those who are tenure-track and clinical. I thought of some of the items we wrote on our discussion sheets: intentional hires of cohorts to lessen tokenism and isolation; providing travel and professional development funding; mentoring, both formal and informal; and how do we decolonize whiteness within a LIS environment on the level of education, recruitment and retention. These are issues that many attendees were looking for the answers to. Having them enumerated was important, but we now need to address them. Having more of us write about the experience will help us to remember and start the process of implementing these doable ideas.

As a seasoned librarian, do you feel it addressed needs you might have as a professional?

I didn't see this as a forum for seasoned librarians; we were more there to be the experts. I'm more interested in how leadership is developed--but also when one is overlooked, what are the steps to file grievance or a lawsuit. What should a seasoned librarian consider when going up for leadership, promotion, or administrative positions? What if the person is more qualified, what are some steps to take for redress? We had a few HR experts, but these were issues that weren't addressed or discussed; they were not the focus either. I do think these are concerns of recruitment, hiring, and retention.

What do you think were the Takeaways from the Forum?

The big takeaway for me was that more dialogue is needed. Research and publishing should be included in the LIS process and we need to tackle some of the issues we listed. There needs to be a corpus of literature about these issues;

---

3 President Obama Announces More Key Administration Posts: https://obamawhitehouse.archives. gov/the-press-office/2016/12/06/president-obama-announces-more-key-administration-posts

they should be studied as any other subject is studied, with solutions and plans developed. We need to understand how we go about getting some of our suggestions implemented. How do they get to the HR professionals and administrators who make the decisions of who to hire and fire? How do we hold folks accountable for moving the needle faster? Research, data gathering, publishing, sharing and engaging with people on multiple levels were all discussed and we should be finding ways of implementing these ideas before we forget. I think we all decided that having another forum that focuses on the implementation stage should be our next step.

How do you think the Forum will be seen by individuals who did not attend?

Hopefully, those folks who did not attend will benefit and add to our discussions and write-up. I loved the fact that our sessions were streamed and that people outside the Forum were able to ask questions and challenge our responses. There are many more of these events, activities, forums, conferences, that SHOULD continue, and I don't expect to be at all of them. We have to pick and choose what we can do. As I am wont to note, there is not one forum or event that will solve or address all of the issues. Communication, discussion, and engagement are the only ways to make a difference and these opportunities will involve more individuals who will continually bring new ideas and solutions.

What do you need to know about the Forum which may not be apparent in the upcoming video or white paper?

The continuing elephant in the room for younger LIS professionals was the feeling that they are in toxic environments, are not appreciated for their skill sets, and the continual revolving door of recruitment and retention of LIS professionals of color. I do think we need more data, research and publishing on these issues. Newer LIS professionals need to know that they are valued and most importantly, that they are not alone! They are often bombarded with conflicting information on what they should or should not do as professionals. As someone who has been interviewed by a number of new LIS professionals my message to them is consistent: get out of your comfort zone, travel, look into Fulbright Fellowships, volunteer (if you have time) with local groups. More importantly, keep yourself open to new ideas, and make diversity, inclusion, cultural competency, and excellence the battles you pick!

Jina DuVernay, Special Collections Librarian at Alabama State University's Levi Watkins Learning Center

What expectations did you have about the Forum? Were your expectations realized? Why or why not?

I expected to collaborate with other librarians to discuss possible remedies for the lack of recruitment and retention of people of color in the library and information science profession. I feel my expectations were met because we did just that. We were encouraged to ask questions and speak to one another about our ideas. Additionally, on the second day of the Forum we were asked to get in groups and we affixed some of our ideas to recruit and retain minorities in the library and information science field on the wall so that all participants could walk around and view each group's ideas. This was a great, interactive way to share a lot of information in a short amount of time. The Forum was organized well and the agenda adhered to the advertised program.

What in your opinion was significant about the Forum?

In my opinion, the venue was significant. The Forum gathered librarians from an array of institutions to discuss issues regarding minorities in the field of Library and Information Science to Hampton University, the first university to offer a Baccalaureate degree in Library Science for African Americans. To have convened on the campus where the first conference was held for African American librarians in 1927 added a deeper significance to our purpose during the Forum. The location prompted a greater sense of pride in my participation in the Forum and in continuing the work of those librarians who preceded me in meeting on the campus of Hampton University at the First Negro Library Conference.

Was it important for the Forum to take place at an HBCU? Why or why not?

It was important for the Forum to take place at an HBCU because the intent of the Forum was to try to identify effective ways in which minorities can and should be recruited and retained in librarianship. An HBCU setting was fitting for a Forum regarding issues of diversity as the premise of HBCUs were to ensure that minorities--specifically African Americans--had access to, and benefitted from an education. In that same vein, minorities need to be and should be included in the LIS profession, so that libraries can effectively serve their communities by employing professionals with varying backgrounds and knowledge. In this way, a diverse staff can more accurately complement a diverse community.

Could the Forum be held anywhere?

The Forum definitely could have been held anywhere. However, meeting on the campus of Hampton University was especially meaningful given the history of the First Negro Library Conference. It felt appropriate to meet at a historically Black university to discuss issues related to minorities. The space inside of the William R. & Norma B. Harvey Library on Hampton University's campus was inviting and warm and conducive to a productive meeting.

Did you think it was important to keep the attendance level low?

I do think that it was important to keep the attendance level low because the smaller group of participants created an intimate setting. This prompted a greater sense of comfort and enabled the group to be more involved during the Forum. A larger number of attendees would have been less likely to achieve this. I thought that the attendees represented library professionals at every stage from library students to seasoned professionals. Having attendees from varying stages in librarianship was beneficial, especially for library directors and human resources professionals. In order for the Forum to determine fair solutions, there had to have been fair representation.

What did you think of the kinds of attendees to the Forum?

I found the "Lunch and Learn Diversity Panel" to be the most meaningful. The expert professionals, Ms. Rebecca Hankins, Dr. Miguel Juárez, and Dr. Nicole Cooke, expounded on issues regarding diversity. Even though most of the experiences that the panelists discussed were ones that occurred in predominantly white work environments, I felt encouraged to know that despite attempts by some to devalue and discredit their work, they were able to forge ahead and thrive in successful careers. Knowing that these challenges are not unique to only those who work in predominantly white spaces, I found the panelists to be quite inspiring.

What do you think was lacking at the Forum?

If there was anything that was lacking in the meeting, I would say that it would have been nice to have more time for the attendees to collaborate. However, the Forum took place over a two-day period, so time was limited. Following the Forum, too, there have been a couple of conference calls and email interactions between the participants.

What would you have done differently?

What I would have done differently was to have allotted some more time for participant interaction, allowing for more in-depth brainstorming. I could have listened to the guest speakers all day. They were entertaining and informative; however, if their talks were more brief, the second half of the first day could have been devoted to rolling up our sleeves and diving right into the brainstorming with our groups. The following day we collaborated most of the day and I think that we made good use of the time that we had to work on drafting ideas to recruit and retain minorities in the LIS field.

As a newer librarian, do you feel it addressed needs you might have as a professional?

As a newer librarian, I felt that it benefited me greatly to hear from more experienced professionals discuss issues that they face in leadership roles regarding their struggle to recruit and/or retain minority professionals. Listening to these librarians gave me a glimpse of some of their concerns as leaders in this profession.

Should I ever find myself in a leadership role in the library, the issue of recruitment and retainment of minority library professionals will not be a surprise. Moreover, it was inspiring to know that they endured challenges of microaggressions in the workplace and yet persevered as they continued their education and careers. This certainly served as a reminder to me that I can do the same.

What do you think were the takeaways from the Forum?

One of the takeaways from the Forum was that there is a definite need for strategic marketing for recruitment purposes. It was suggested that librarianship needed to be on the radar of young students and thought of as a desirable profession. Another takeaway was that mentoring is key in order to retain minority professionals. These ideas are important ways in which the library and information science field can attract and maintain minority library professionals.

How do you think the Forum will be seen by individuals who did not attend? What do you need to know about the Forum which may not be apparent in the upcoming video or white paper?

I think that the Hampton LIS Forum will be seen as a fantastic start to a very relevant and necessary conversation. What may not be apparent from the video or white paper is the camaraderie that existed during the Forum. It provided an excellent opportunity to network, specifically with experienced librarians whose work I have followed and admired. Everyone that I interacted with shared a positiveness and likemindedness that was tremendously refreshing for me. Being chosen after competing to participate in meaningful work designed for a select few, was very thrilling. I left feeling hopeful, inspired and honored to be have been selected to participate in the Forum. The connections that I made during the Forum have proved to be invaluable. It was an experience that I will not soon forget.

Artwork by Shanalee Hampton
www.shanaleehampton.com

Contributors

Melissa Cardenas-Dow

Melissa Cardenas-Dow is a social sciences librarian at Sacramento State University. She is currently a co-chair of the American Library Association Equity, Diversity & Inclusion Implementation Working Group (2016-2019), a member of the 2019 ALA Nominating Committee, Co-Editor of the ALA Social Responsibilities Round Table Newsletter (2014-2020), and a Councilor-at-Large. Most recently, she worked with the Joint Conference of Librarians of Color (JCLC) as the Graphics Design Coordinator within the JCLC 2018 Public Relations Committee.

Andrea Castillo

As an adult services librarian in Alexandria, Virginia, I wear book recommender, computer troubleshooter and program planner hats, hosting Spanish conversation hours, death cafes and a Wikipedia editing workshop, among other events. I am a 2017-2018 American Libraries Association Spectrum Scholar, and my work appears in Jen Golbeck's 2018 book Online Harassment. In another life, I was a newspaper reporter in Georgia and Virginia, writing about education, crime, weather, religion, entertainment, food and everything in between. I received a Georgia Press Association award for investigative reporting in 2014 and was named a

Chips Quinn Scholar in 2011. I believe that both my former profession and my current, at their best, empower others through information. I'm an alumna of Northwestern University and the University of Maryland, and I also have a graduate certificate in aging and applied thanatology from the University of Maryland, Baltimore. I'm a proud Cubarican (Cuban + Puerto Rican American) who enjoys knitting, bad puns, obscure trivia and obsessing over my curly hair.

Carmen A. Collins

Carmen is passionate about education, helping underrepresented populations with digital resources and advancing technology to improve processes. She is a graduate of the University of Maryland where she obtained a Masters in Science in Information and Library Science with a concentration in Archives and Digital Curation. Currently, she works as an Information Analyst for Tesla Government Solutions. She lives in Severna Park, MD, with her two daughters and husband. Some of her interests include crafting, politics, puzzles, trivia, reading, running, as well as spending quality time with family and friends. One day she would like to be a contestant on the game show Jeopardy!

Jina DuVernay

Jina DuVernay is the Special Collections Librarian at Alabama State University's Levi Watkins Learning Center and serves on the Steering Committee for ASU's National Center for the Study of Civil Rights and African American Culture. DuVernay proudly serves on the board of the Black Caucus American Library Association and the Black Heritage Council of the Alabama Historical Commission. She is also a member of the Coretta Scott King Book Awards Committee and the Alabama Book Festival Committee. She holds a Master of Liberal Arts and a Master of Library and Information Science. DuVernay's research interests include community outreach and engagement and diversity in libraries.

Rebecca Hankins

Rebecca Hankins is an Associate Professor and a certified archivist/ librarian. She has been at Texas A & M University since 2003, receiving tenure in 2010. She was elected to the prestigious Society of American Archivists' Distinguished Fellows in 2016 and holds the Wendler Endowed Professorship at Texas A&M University's Libraries. In December of 2016, U. S. President Barack Hussein Obama appointed her to the National Historical Publications and Records Commission (NHPRC), the funding arm of the National Archives and Records Administration (NARA), a 3-year position. Her research intersects with her professional work that centers on the African Diaspora, Women & Gender Studies, and the use of popular culture as a pedagogical methodology that offers new approaches to the study of Islam. In 2016 her book, co-authored with Miguel Juarez, Ph. D., was published by Library Juice Press titled "Where are All the Librarians of Color: The Experiences of People of Color in Academia."

Dr. Miguel Juárez

Dr. Miguel Juárez received his MLS degree from the State University of New York at Buffalo in 1998, as part of the Arthur A. Schomburg Library Residency Program. He has a BA in Liberal Arts, and an additional MA and PhD in Borderlands History from the University of Texas at El Paso. He worked as an academic librarian/archivist from 1999 to 2013 at the State University of New York at Buffalo; at the University of Arizona Main Library and at the Center for Creative Photography Library; at the Cushing Memorial Library and Archives at Texas A&M University; at the Chicano Studies Research Center at UCLA; at El Paso Community College; and at the University of North Texas. He has published two books: Where Are All the Librarians of Color: The Experiences of People of Color in Academia, co-edited with Rebecca Hankins (2015, Library Juice Press); and Colors on Desert Walls: The Murals of El Paso, (1997, Texas Western Press). His articles have appeared in: Arts Documentation, The Bulletin of the Art Libraries Society of North America; The El Paso Times; the El Paso Herald Post; Latino Rebels; Fusion Magazine; MujeresTalkblog; the Borderlands History blog; Newsies.us; and in CultureWork: A Periodic Broadside for

Arts & Culture Workers; and in Somos Primos. He has written chapters and articles in the following books: The Power of Language/El Poder de la Palabra: Selected Papers from the Second REFORMA National Conference; Ordinary Women, Extraordinary Lives: American Women's History; Diversity in Libraries: Academic Residency Programs; and in Where Are All the Librarians of Color. He is an adjunct professor in the Department of History at the University of Texas at El Paso and in the Department of ESL, Reading and Social Sciences at the El Paso El Paso Community College and serves on the editorial board of Latinx Talk, an online, interdisciplinary, peer-reviewed, and moderated forum, https://latinxtalk.org/.

Liz Laribee

I am an Education Specialist with the Smithsonian Libraries. As an illustrator and arts advocate, launched The MakeSpace Arts Collective, Sprocket Mural Arts, and DCBA Lawyers for the Arts in Harrisburg, PA. I have been granted the Spectrum Arts Award, the YWCA Emerging Leader Award, and the title of Artist in Residence for the City of Harrisburg. My illustration work has appeared in Colonial Comics (Fulcrum, 2018) and Occasionally Accurate Science (Nomadic Press, 2019), and I have been interviewed about various creative projects by The Huffington Post, ColorLines, Inside Higher Ed, and the American Library Association. I live in Virginia, happily. www.lizlaribee.com

Erica Soto

Erica Soto graduated with her Bachelor's Degree in Psychology in 2017. During her academic career she began working as a Library Page, was promoted to Clerical Aide, and soon after became Library Assistant of her local library system. With over 10 years of experience in early childhood development, her deep passion for literacy, education, community engagement and resource connection allows her to advocate for the most vulnerable communities in various ways. She is a graduate of the Latino Talent Initiative of Ferris University, a cohort designed to strengthen and empower young Latinx professionals and leaders. Erica serves on the leadership team of the City of Grand Rapids Neighborhood Summit as Kids Summit Coordinator. She is a member of the Latina Network of West Michigan and the LEAD Program for Parents of and Individuals with Special Needs. She is currently transitioning from serving as Marketing and Communications Co-Chair to President Elect of BL²END, a local non-profit organization that intentionally creates environments of inclusion for Young Professionals of Color, monthly, and focuses on the strategic initiatives of Professional Development, Social Networking, and Community Outreach. She also provides consultation services for organizations and schools, connecting them to vital community resources and partners. She was recently recognized for her leadership and named one of the 2018 Top 50 Latinas in Michigan by the Hispanic/Latino Commission of Michigan.Erica is a proud single mother of 3 and currently works as a Bilingual Educator for the inner city Grand Rapids Public School system.

Grace Yamada

Grace Yamada is a librarian and poet born in Alberta, Canada and raised in New York City. She earned a B.A from New York University in 2014 and graduated from the Palmer School of Library Science in 2016. She currently works for the New York Public Library, focusing on learning technology and digital literacies for young adults. She served on the NYPL Best Books for Teens Committee 2017-2018. An Intern and Docent at the Lesbian Herstory Archive since 2016, Grace works with preserve and promote the collection. She also works as head dramaturge and communications director of the Constellation Project, theatre collective promoting science fiction in the arts. An emerging poet, her work is published in Leopardskin's Limes.

Max Macias, Yago Cura, Rani Macias, , Carmen A. Collins, Dolly Martino, Sheila Garcia , Angelo Moreno, Nephtali Gomez, Judy Lee, Jason K. Alston & Autumn Anglin

Above: Photograph by Crystal Burgoyne from the Interfaith Sunday Service, Sheridan Federal Prision, I.C.E. detention facility, Oregon, June 24, 2018, photograph used with permission .

Below: Photograph by Crystal Burgoyne from the Interfaith Sunday Service, Sheridan Federal Prision, I.C.E. detention facility, Oregon, June 24, 2018, photograph used with permission .

Artist Bios

Libidoart

Libidoart (she/her) is an artist currently residing in Seattle, Washington.
Her work focuses on body positivity and sexual/sensual positivity. Her most
influential and favorite artist is Ghada Amer.
Libidoart is inspired by street art and has included her messages by getting it out
there- in the streets from the Pacific Northwest to Tehran, Iran.
She has shown her work in galleries in Portland, Oregon; Seattle, Washington
and participated in the first Feminist Art Festival in Amsterdam.
https://www.libidobidil.com/

Crystal Burgoyne

Born in Boise, ID
Lives & works in Oregon & Colorado,
United States

Crystal Burgoyne is an artist who employs photography as a means for exploring
issues of identity and social justice. She pursues opportunities to photograph
demonstrations of activism in an attempt to understand what participating
in democracy looks like. Her most recent conceptual photography series is an
exploration of the sense of self through self-portraiture. She deals with themes of
censorship and digital privacy, institutionalized oppression, environmental and
social justice, and motherhood.

Born in Boise, Idaho, Burgoyne moved to Oregon in 1997. She holds a degree in
Environmental Studies from Willamette University and a Post-Baccalaureate
of Craft in Fine Art Photography from Oregon College of Art and Craft. She
maintains studios in Oregon and Colorado.

Shanalee Hampton

Find out more about Shanalee on her website. www.shanaleehampton.com.

Appendix A

"Podium" by Yago Cura (HINCHAS Press, 2018)

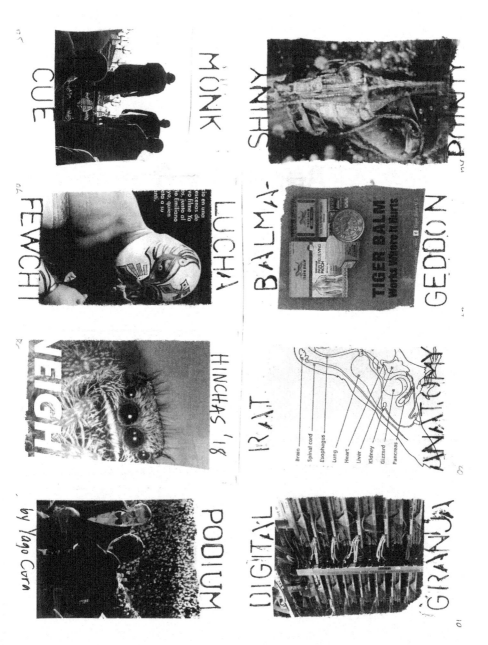

Appendix B

Instructions/Graphics for a 6-Fold Zine

How to fold a zine

By www.tellatale.org.uk

Appendix C

Activity for Hampton LIS Forum Lunch and Learn

Library Report Card

(Please do not self-identify yourself or your institution)

Fold in rules of engagement – this activity is meant to be anonymous. This is a safe space, but be mindful of live-streaming.

Using a scale from A+, A, A-, B+, B, B-, C+, C, C-, D+, D, D- or F:

How would you rate your university on fair and equitable diversity? _____

How would you rate the climate at your institution (and not the weather)? _____

Do you agree with the statement that there are issues of privilege in libraries? _____

If you were the supreme power, what would you change about your institution? _____

Above: Photograph by Crystal Burgoyne from the Interfaith Sunday Service, Sheridan Federal Prision, I.C.E. detention facility, Oregon, June 24, 2018, photograph used with permission .

Below: Photograph by Crystal Burgoyne from the Families Together Rally, Salem Oregon, June 30, 2018, photograph used with permission .

References

DIGITAL CITIZENSHIP IN ITS SECOND DECADE: AN EXAMINATION AND A WAY FORWARD

Altınay Gazi, Z. (2016). Internalization of Digital Citizenship for the Future of All Levels of Education. TED EĞİTİM VE BİLİM, 41(186).

Atif, Yacine, and Chien Chou. "Digital Citizenship: Innovations in Education, Practice, and Pedagogy." Journal of Educational Technology & Society, vol. 21, no. 1, 2018, pp.152–154. JSTOR, JSTOR, www.jstor.org/stable/26273876.

Domonoske, Camila. "Students Have 'Dismaying' Inability To Tell Fake News From Real, Study Finds." NPR, NPR, 23 Nov. 2016.

Finlayson, J. G. (2005). Habermas: A very short introduction. Oxford: Oxford University Press.

Geiger, A. (2017, June 21). Millennials are the most likely generation of Americans to use public libraries.

Horrigan, John B. "Libraries 2016." Pew Research Center: Internet, Science & Tech, Pew Research Center, 9 Sept. 2016, www.pewinternet.org/2016/09/09/libraries-2016.

Joint, Nicholas. "Democracy, eLiteracy and the internet." Library Review, Feb. 2005, p.80+.

Mossberger, K., Tolbert, C. J., & McNeal, R. S. (2010). Digital citizenship: The Internet, society, and participation. Cambridge, Mass.: MIT Press.

Noble, S. U. (2018). Algorithms of oppression: How search engines reinforce racism. New York: New York University Press.

Pedersen, Alex Young, et al. "Patterns of Inclusion: Fostering Digital

Citizenship through Hybrid Education." Journal of Educational Technology & Society, vol. 21, no. 1, 2018, pp. 225–236. JSTOR, www.jstor.org/stable/26273882.

Ribble, Mike S., and Gerald D. Bailey. "Monitoring technology misuse & abuse: a five- step plan for creating a digital citizenship program in your school." T H E Journal [Technological Horizons In Education], Aug. 2004, p. 22+.

Searson, M., Hancock, M., Soheil, N. and Shepherd, G. (2015). Digital citizenship within global contexts. Education and Information Technologies, 20(4), pp.729-741.

Van Deursen, A. J., & Van Dijk, J. A. (2010). Dijk Internet Skills and the Digital Divide. New Media & Society, 13(6). Retrieved April 03, 2018.

SENIOR CITIZEN ZINESTERS

Heimlich, R. (2010). Baby Boomers Retire [Pew Research]. Retrieved from http://www.pew research.org/fact-tank/2010/12/29/baby-boomers-retire/

La GANGA, M.,L. (1994, Jan 03). COLUMN ONE telling all with wit and rage personal zines are self-published glimpses into the lives of twentysomethings. those with a touch of the voyeur can follow the details of romance, tragedy and the bizarre. Los Angeles Times (Pre-1997 Fulltext) Retrieved from http://ezproxy.lapl.org/login?   url=https://search-proquest-com.ezproxy.lapl.org/docview/282151502?accountid=6749

Rowe, Chip, editor. The Book of Zines: Readings from the Fringe. Henry Holt, NYC: 1997.

Sutin, A. R., Stephan, Y., Luchetti, M., & Terracciano, A. (October 26, 2018). Loneliness and Risk of Dementia. The Journals of Gerontology: Series B.

REMEMBERING CONSCIOUSNESS IS POWER: WORKING TO CENTER ACADEMIC LIBRARY OUTREACH IN THE SERVICE OF SOCIAL JUSTICE, ASIAN PACIFIC AMERICAN ETHNIC VISIBILITY, AND COALITION-BUILDING

Absher, L. U., & Cardenas-Dow, M. (2016). Collaborative Librarianship: A Minority Opinion. Collaborative Librarianship, 8(4). Retrieved from: https://digitalcommons.du.edu/collaborativelibrarianship/vol8/iss4/3

Bishop, A. & Moffat, K. (2017). Experiencing whiteness of LIS education: An autoethnographic account. In Y. Cura & M. Macias (Eds.), Librarians with Spines: Information agitators in an age of stagnation (pp 3-21). San Bernardino, CA: Createspace.

Bonnet, J. & McAlexander, B. (2012). Structural diversity in academic libraries: A study of librarian approachability. Journal of Academic Librarianship 38(5), 277-286.

Cardenas-Dow, M. (2013, January). APA library leader interview – Judy Lee, Riverside, California. Apalaweb. Retrieved from: http:// http://www.apalaweb.org/apa-libraryleader-interview-judy-lee-riverside-california/

Clarke, J. H., Pun, R., & Tong, M. (Eds.). (2018). Asian American librarians and library services: Activism, Collaborations, and Strategies. Lanham, MD: Rowman & Littlefield.

Collins, J.C. (2001). Good to great: why some companies make the leap... and others don't. New York, NY: HarperBusiness.

Colmenar, G. (2018). Doing the work you want your library to do: Reflections of an academic librarian. In J. H. Clarke, R. Pun, & M. Tong (Eds.), Asian American librarians and library services: Activism, collaborations, and strategies (pp. 291-306). Lanham, MD: Rowman & Littlefield.

Deitering, A., Schroeder, R., & Stoddart, R. (Eds.). (2017). The self as subject: Autoethnographic research into identity, culture, and academic librarianship. Chicago, IL: Association of College and Research Libraries.

Deitering, A. (2017). Why autoethnography? In A. Deitering, R. Schroeder, & R. Stoddart (Eds.), The self as subject, Autoethnographic research into identity, culture, and academic librarianship (pp. 1-22). Chicago, IL: Association of College and Research Libraries.

Ellis, C., Adams, T. E, & Bochner, A. P. (2010). Autoethnography: An overview. Forum Qualitative Sozialforschung / Forum: Qualitative Social Research, 12(1). doi: http://dx.doi.org/10.17169/fqs-12.1.159

Grant, A. (2013). Give and take: A revolutionary approach to success. New York, NY: Viking.

Hollander, J. (2015, October 5). 9 Grace Lee Boggs Feminist Quotes That Will Inspire You To Smash Through the Glass Ceiling, Too. Retrieved from https://www.bustle.com/articles/115047-9-grace-lee-boggs-feminist-quotes-that-will-inspire-you-to-smash-through-the-glass-ceiling

Komisar, R. (2001). The monk and the riddle: the art of creating a life while making a living. Boston, MA: Harvard Business School Press.

Lankes, R. D. (2011). The atlas of new librarianship. Cambridge, MA: MIT Press.

Lee, E. & Yung, J. (2010). Angel Island: immigrant gateway to America. New York, NY: Oxford University Press.

Lowe, F. (Producer and Director). (2015). Chinese Couplets [DVD]. San Francisco, CA: Lowedown Productions.

Ng, K. (2016, August 3). That Random Asian Guy. Retrieved from http://blog.angryasianman.com/2016/08/that-random-asian-guy.html

Ni, C. (2010, January 24) A family delves into the mystery of a 'paper son': a Chinese immigrant's secret is uncovered only after his death. Los Angeles Times. Retrieved from https://www.pressreader.com/usa/los-angeles-times/20100124/281964603852676; also from http://www.steveyeeartifacts.com/100224LATimes.pdf.

Ni, C. (2010, January 24). A Chinese American Immigration Secret Emerges from the Dark Days of Discrimination. Los Angeles Times. Retrieved from http://articles.latimes.com/2010/jan/24/local/la-me-paper-son24-2010jan24

Reale, M. (2017). Becoming a reflective librarian and teacher: Strategies for mindful academic practice. Chicago, IL: ALA editions, an imprint of the American Library Association.

Schroeder, R. (2017) Evaluative criteria for autoethnographic research: Who's to judge? In A. Deitering, R. Schroeder, & R. Stoddart (Eds.), The self as subject, Autoethnographic research into identity, culture, and academic librarianship (pp. 1-22). Chicago, IL: Association of College and Research Libraries.

Simmons, M. (2013, July 22). If you want to go fast, go alone. If you want to go far, go together. Forbes.com. Retrieved from: https://www.forbes.com/sites/ michaelsimmons/2013/07/22/power-of-relational-thinking/#51f2589710e3

Yamaguchi, H. (2018). Asian Americans and libraries: Anthology authors talk about identity, erasure, and inclusion. American Libraries Magazine. Retrieved from: https://americanlibrariesmagazine.org/blogs/the-scoop/asian-americans-and-libraries/

Zhang, Q. (2010). Asian Americans beyond the model minority stereotype: The nerdy and the left out. Journal of International and Intercultural Communication, 3(1), 20-37.

AMIRA IN AMERICA

American Library Association. (2018, April 06). Winners of the 2018 Will Eisner Graphic Novel Grants for Libraries announced. Retrieved June 6, 2018, from; http://www.ala.org/news/press-releases/2018/04/winners-2018-will-eisner-graphic-novel-grants-libraries-announced

Anderman, E. M., & Maehr, M. L. (1994). Motivation and schooling in the middle grades. Review of educational Research, 64(2), 287–309.

Bell, S. J., & Shank, J. (2004). The blended librarian: A blueprint for redefining the teaching and learning role of academic librarians. College & Research Libraries News, 65(7), 372-375. doi:10.5860/crln.65.7.7297

Bishop, R.S. (1990). Mirrors, windows, and sliding glass doors. Perspectives, 6(3), ix–xi.

Bishop, R.S. (2012). Reflections on the development of African American children's literature. Journal of Children's Literature, 38(2), 5–13.

Carleton, S. (2014, Spring). Drawn to Change: Comics and Critical Consciousness. Retrieved May 30, 2018, from http://www.lltjournal.ca/index. php/llt/article/view/5782

Casey, H. (2012). Multimodal Learning Clubs. Middle School Journal,

44(2), 39-48. doi:10.1080/00940771.2012.11461846

Dawes, N. P. & Larson, R. (2011). How youth get engaged: Grounded-theory research on motivational development in organized youth programs. Developmental Psychology, 47(1), 259–269.

Doherty, J. J. (2007, June). No Shhing: Giving Voice to the Silenced: An Essay in Support of Critical Information Literacy. Retrieved May 30, 2018, from https://digitalcommons.unl.edu/libphilprac/133/

Fazel, M., Reed, R. V., Panter-Brick, C., & Stein, A. (2012). Mental health of displaced and refugee children resettled in high-income countries: Risk and protective factors. The Lancet, 379(9812), 266-282. doi:10.1016/s0140-6736(11)60051-2

"FY 2015 Served Populations by State and Country of Origin (all Served Populations)." Office   of Refugee Resettlement. N.p., 22 Apr. 2016. Web. 22 Oct. 2016.

Garcia, K. (n.d.). Keeping Up With... Critical Librarianship. Retrieved June 6, 2018, from http://www.ala.org/acrl/publications/keeping_up_with/critlib

Godfrey, Sarah. "As Public Libraries Embrace Maker Rooms, Are the Poorest Users Being Left Behind?" Washington Post. N.p., 31 Mar. 2016. Web. 22 Oct. 2016.

Harter, S., Whitesell, N. R., & Kowalski, P. (1992). Individual differences in the effects of educational transitions on young adolescents' perceptions of competence and motivational orientation. American Educational Research Journal, 29(4), 777–807.

Jacobs, D. (2013). Graphic encounters : comics and the sponsorship of multimodal literacy. Retrieved from https://ebookcentral.proquest.com

Kobel, P. S. (n.d.). Ethiopian Americans. Retrieved November 13, 2016, from http://www.everyculture.com/multi/Du-Ha/Ethiopian-Americans.html.

"Library Services: Immigration & Citizenship." The Hartford Public Library. N.p., n.d. Web. 23 Oct. 2016.

Lloyd, A., Kennan, M. A., Thompson, K. M., & Qayyum, A. (2013). Connecting with new information landscapes: Information literacy practices of refugees. Journal of Documentation, 69(1), 121-144. doi:10.1108/00220411311295351.

Mills, K.A. & Unsworth, L. (2017). iPad Animations: Powerful Multimodal Practices for Adolescent Literacy and Emotional Language. Journal of Adolescent & Adult Literacy, 61(6), 609–620. doi: 10.1002/jaal.717

Nyberg, A. K. (2010). How Librarians Learned to Love the Graphic Novel in R.G. Weiner (Ed.) Graphic Novels and Comics in Libraries and Archives. Retrieved May 30, 2018, from https://books.google.com/books?id=Xo-QYdfL9DoC&lpg=PA26&ots=dVcaC-F-3m&lr&pg=PA26#v=onepage&q&f=false

"Outreach Resources for Services to People of Color." American Library Association. N.p., n.d.   Web. 23 Oct. 2016.

Refugee arrival data. (2015, November 24). Office of Refugee Resettlement. Retrieved October 11, 2016, from http://www.acf.hhs.gov/orr/resource/refugee-arrival-data.

Schwarz, G. (2006). Expanding Literacies through Graphic Novels. English Journal, 95(6), 58. doi:10.2307/30046629

Ten Years of Language Access in Washington, DC. (n.d.). Retrieved November 23, 2016, from https://www.urban.org/research/publication/ten-years-language-access-washington-dc/view/full_report

Thomas Juneau, Mira Sucharov; Narratives in Pencil: Using Graphic Novels to Teach Israeli-Palestinian Relations, International Studies Perspectives, Volume 11, Issue 2, 1 May 2010, Pages 172–183, https://doi-org.proxy-um.researchport.umd.edu/10.1111/j.1528-3585.2010.00400.x

Tschida, C., Ryan, C., & Ticknor, A. (2014). Building on windows and mirrors: Encouraging the disruption of "Single stories" through children's literature. Journal of Children's Literature, 40(1), 28-39.

Tyrer, R. A., & Fazel, M. (2014). School and community-based interventions for refugee and asylum seeking children: a systematic review. Plos One. Retrieved from http://dx.doi.org/10.1371/journal.pone.0089359

UNICEF USA. (2016, March 15). How Syrian Children Cope — Saja Tells Her Story. Children Of Syria Speak. Retrieved November 29, 2016, from https://www.unicefusa.org/stories/how-syrian-children-cope-—-saja-tells-her-story/30094.

TAKEAWAYS FROM THE HAMPTON LIS FORUM

Beveridge, Andrew A. et. al. Librarians in the United States from 1880-2009. Oxford University Press's Academic Insights for the Thinking World. June 20th, 2011. Reviewed 1-10-19, https://blog.oup.com/2011/06/librarian-census/

Caldera, M. A., & Neal, K. M. (Eds.). (2018). Through the Archival Looking Glass: A Reader on Diversity and Inclusion. Chicago, IL: ALA Editions.

Cooke, N. A. (2017, May 4). Tolerance Is Not Good Enough. Retrieved from https://lj.libraryjournal.com/2017/05/opinion/backtalk/tolerance-is-not-good-enough-backtalk.

Cooke, N. A. (2017). Information Services to Diverse Populations: Developing Culturally Competent Library Professionals. Santa Barbara, CA: Libraries Unlimited, an imprint of ABC-CLIO, LLC.

Hampton University Forum on Minority Recruitment and Retention in the LIS Field (August 2018) https://hamptonu.libguides.com/c.php?g=815577&p=5825161

Hankins, R., & Juárez, M. (2015). Where are all The Librarians of Color? The Experiences of People of Color in Academia. Sacramento, CA: Library Juice Press.

Hathcock, A. (2015, October 7). White Librarianship in Blackface: Diversity Initiatives in LIS. Retrieved from http://www.inthelibrarywiththeleadpipe.org/2015/lis-diversity/

President Obama Announces More Key Administration Posts: https://obamawhitehouse.archives.gov/the-press-office/2016/12/06/president-obama-announces-more-key-administration-posts

References

Artwork by Shanalee Hampton
www.shanaleehampton.com

Index

52446856R00086

Made in the USA
Middletown, DE
10 July 2019